Power of Positive Impact

Using the Little Things
to Make a Difference

Dr. Love Otuechere

iUNIVERSE, INC.
BLOOMINGTON

Power of Positive Impact
Using the Little Things to Make a Difference

iUniverse books may be ordered through booksellers or by contacting:

iUniverse
1663 Liberty Drive
Bloomington, IN 47403
www.iuniverse.com
1-800-Authors (1-800-288-4677)

Because of the dynamic nature of the Internet, any web addresses or links contained in this book may have changed since publication and may no longer be valid. The views expressed in this work are solely those of the author and do not necessarily reflect the views of the publisher, and the publisher hereby disclaims any responsibility for them.

Any people depicted in stock imagery provided by Thinkstock are models, and such images are being used for illustrative purposes only.

Certain stock imagery © Thinkstock.

ISBN: 978-1-4759-4543-0 (sc)
ISBN: 978-1-4759-4544-7 (hc)
ISBN: 978-1-4759-4545-4 (e)

Library of Congress Control Number: 2012914940

Printed in the United States of America

iUniverse rev. date: 9/13/2012

Dedication

For Everyone out there that is taking time to make a difference in the lives of others. There is grace in your hands and glitter in your eyes from Heaven as parents to make sacrifices in love for restoration of dignity, purpose in our communities.

Contents

An Effective Model for the Recovery and Development of a Society: An Individual Makes a Difference Even with Little

Positive impact is a powerful force within all individuals to respond to problems, needs, and situations. The development and growth in the economy and society are dependent on this impact. Positive impact is one of God's recipes for lifting up, providing hope and meaningful services to oneself and others. This lifestyle fosters good thoughts to project enthusiasm, remove doubts, and create positive outcomes of delivery and learning systems via inputs. Our world is so broad, and an individual's disposition to meet all needs is so limited. One needs others to advance to receive advice to services, and to impact and develop skills for use to serve in various capacities. Everyone has something to offer in order to bring meaning to life. People are needed to interpret policies and to provide guidance via technical, physical, and emotional support.

Evidence of a lack of employment, great disparity in wages, and gaps in connectivity is proof that we need to work hard to impact each other for mutual benefits. We are not using our unique attributes to help others to hope, dream, and aspire higher. Society is responsible for developing the skills needed to cater for its development and needs. Thus, any investment made to develop new technology and to improve the services of professionals to impact the people will always help society to move ahead. This is the reason why people who take time to study the needs of their environment, and who align their careers and plan their future to meet those needs, are always ahead and doing better in life.

Every human has so much untapped knowledge, words of encouragement, and skill that he or she can give out to others during his or her lifetime. A failure to do so is due to not knowing, not caring, or being selfish. You may also be exposed to people and things that are not meant for you, or for operating outside your destined territory. You are a vessel full of substance and inner will to impact, receive, and give out freely, emptying yourself to serve others with no reservation. Your positive impact is your masterpiece display of compassion, kindness, words of encouragement, noble services, and aid to others to derive fulfillment and wealth in return. This meaningful impact to make a difference will not only determine your next level of upward mobility, but it will always enlist your name in the heart of people you touched.

The importance of good relationships and team spirit are the keys to securing victorious, prosperous, healthy, and peaceful paths; these ideas have been outlined and demonstrated in the Creator's manual. It is very obvious that everybody wants a wealthy, long life, having peace and becoming successful. However, people's view on working their way to attain these goals is tinted for not taking time to learn the steps and the process of a successful journey in life. The ultimate point is that God created you to have a prosperous life using the transformative power of love, and you have a burden to make a difference, whereby you look out for others no matter the location, situation, and circumstance. You are designed with unique features and attributes to reach out and touch others for your breakthrough. Your customized personal attributes can remain dormant and unused, thereby making you uncomfortable for not emptying out what you have within. Self-centeredness is a retarding force against reaching out. Selfishness will always keep you mute, silencing your voice's ability to reach others. Your failure to recognize and work out on it may ruin your opportunities to use this platform to broaden your horizon for noble influence and popularity. Out of selfishness, greed and manipulation, one can overlook the interest of others and can develop an abuse of power, systems, and others, which can lead to losing everything for which you have worked.

Your perspective in life will always shift to neglect positive impact, the source of real wealth, when you shift your focus to self-attainment and enrichment, putting others on the back burner. There is nothing wrong with improving yourself to provide better services and have better relationships. However, it becomes a problem when you make it a goal to run a relay race solo just to maximize profit, climb the corporate ladder, and neglect those around you in the process. Watching your actions and their effects on others is very important—your future, happiness, and how you will be remembered are dependent on them. A little encouraging word of a teacher to a struggling student facing a crisis at home could stimulate the student to bounce back and become the research oncologist who finds the cure for cancer.

The attitude to make a difference in the lives of people around you should begin at home, whereby a trusting, supportive, and noncompetitive environment is created to transcend to society at large. The assurance and confidence derived from a supportive home leaves an imprint that enables one to navigate life and to embrace changes, making contributions using information, feedback, and team spirit as a platform to build up. A broad embracement of others' trust, love, gifts, talents, services, and impact is God's recipe for victorious living. The stimulus package to live a victorious life is included in your positive impact for others. This involves the use of your talents, skills, services, words, or actions to stimulate others to hope, when you ignite the deeming light via your impact. This stimulation can be done anywhere, anytime, and to anyone you come across; it is a sure way to obtain enthusiasm, knowledge, drive, and scalability to improve your environment, leaving it buoyant, vibrant, developed, and enriched with a sure return on investment for meaningful services. Your positive impact during your productive years will become your savings in the later years in the form of wages, royalties, and memories from the people you touched.

It is never too late to begin this impact journey to live in wealth, peace, wellness, and fulfillment. Your impact is that hope fulfilled by making a difference as you celebrate the future by enabling others to hope with what you have. This book will help explore various ways to achieve this milestone and to redeem lost time from lessons as you realize that many people have fallen, and it is only through the outstretched hands of others that they were able get back on their feet. Your positive impact is your vehicle into the future; your deeds and other little things done here transport you to your next level. It is the most soothing and happiest thing to do in our joint effort to have a buoyant, developed, peaceful, healthy, and wealthy society.

A Generous Mind Is a Portal to Think about Others and to Succeed

Your mind is a storage area and network to process past and present information analytically, as well as to stay connected, manage time, and grow relationships, business, and family for success. An informed mind senses and receives high-speed visual, graphic, auditory, and physical signals to support daily decision making. A renewed mind is a storage network with the infra-ability to receive visions from the Creator. You are uniquely made to solve problems, mature with patience, and encounter assigned problems to move from one level to another. You will go through challenges when you have something to offer that can impact generations.

Ruth was able to discern her purpose to withstand initial trials and challenges, and that paid off by her marrying Boaz, a rich man from whose lineage Christ was born. Ruth was a Moabite who rejected her pagan way of life by hanging around the people of Israel (Ruth 1–3). A renewed mind is provided with help, nurturing, guidance, protection, and ideas on how to gainfully go about making impact (Gal. 6:9). In short, your victory in life is dependent on how you are able to use the information processed in your mind to solve problems. The ability to make choices is given to you by God. Important elemental ingredients in your information package are warning signs of danger, power, and adverse effects of fear, as well as the power of your words to drive or thwart your impact. It is your choice if you use, abuse, reject, or ignore the information that guides you in the Bible (Jer. 33:3).

The lesson learned from Ruth's story is that your mind is an information warehouse fed with what you hear, read, and experience, and this warehouse forms your belief system. This medium needs to be sound, alert, and healthy in order to always remind you that you are vital and valuable to yourself before you can value people and things around you. This sense of value builds your confidence, dignity, integrity, discipline, and hope to engage the self. All around prosperity is God's will and plan for you. However, your will and plan have to align with His to receive the blueprint and to broaden your horizon. When you know your purpose and are willing to pursue it, then material wealth, health, a long life, and peace are added as bonuses. Your lack of understanding that you have been given the authority to make important decisions on earth can create fear (John 3:31). Fear may resonate when a person lacks the capability to use the information in his or her storage area network to manage the environment. Fear is a virus in the host environment, and God's words are the anti-viral tools. Your Citrix access is the Holy Spirit, automatically harbored by those who believe in Christ. However, the conscience is a general access, available to everyone else to make choices. Citrix access empowers you to fight fear and obtain vital information from your spiritual smart phone (Ps. 32:8–9).

Your mind is programmed to use analytical networks to solve problems in alignment with your scope of purpose. When your vision is clouded for thinking only of how to meet your needs selfishly, the aftermath may not be pleasing (Luke 18:18–27). You are created to broaden your horizon, using the overflow to impact others. Your mind is not meant for fantasy, negativity, or idleness, but for creating a connectivity portal in order to make progress. Your connectivity needs to be checked if you are not prospering and enriching yourself. God's word is the light and food of life. A lack of God's words to discern, visualize, and plant in fertile grounds causes lack, poverty, and unfulfillment. An encounter with Christ removes every spiritual blindness and greed (John 9:25); it provides opportunities to do little things one day at a time faithfully, for gigantic results with time. The encounter also provides a field guide to enable you to pick the right seed, field, season, and vineyard for a great return on investment. Your vision and impact assessment will be mapped out for you when you listen to the Holy Spirit within you. You are God's overflow, as His temple. The body of Christ is a temple equipped to rise above the threshold and to impact others by love, actions, kindness, and giving (Ezek. 47:1–12).

It is unrealistic to think that you will not encounter problems for being successful. Successful people attract envy or attacks, but they have a partnership with an Advocate that sees in secrets and fights for them. Thus, it is wise for anyone who wants to make any kind of dent in this life to seek divine help, security, and a field guide from an Advocate, Jesus Christ for health, living will, and durable power of attorney (Prov. 2:8). Obtaining your vision from God opens doors for connectivity and impact; it enables you to see abundance in lack, joy in adversity, hope in a hopeless situation, and love in hate. The lack of the above causes you to see the opposite during your trial, and you'll use the wrong choice of words and lose out.

Your mind is a repository of unlimited information purposefully designed to reach targeted audience, clients and people via noble services for wealth.

A Loving and Caring Heart Will Never Go Broke

The kindness and brokenness of a loving heart generates a fuel to regenerate lost hope, joy, beauty, purpose, and passion in others; this fuel is caused by disappointments and other external factors. Love is the building block of every home, institution, and society. Every created thing will fade away with time due to lack of maintenance, attention, and genuine love of the people meant to care for it. With care and adequate attention, created things will be desirable, attractive, appealing, tasteful, admired, and cherished. God loves all His creations to have a vested interest in anyone who practices genuine love by going the extra mile for the sake of others. God reciprocates and holds in the highest esteem the effort of anyone who goes beyond the call of duty to maintain a happy, peaceful, productive, and unified environment (Ps. 51). The need to have loving people in every home and entity is imminent when people, nations, and societies are facing various storms and challenges. Genuine love puts the needs of others in perspective with the earnest desire to have these needs met. Loving and kind people have a tendency to calm the storms using special effects; they cause others to hope and to see the good in bad situations, providing helping hands to those who have fallen by the wayside. Anyone can fall by the wayside, either by making poor choices or from the domino effect of others' decisions.

It is evident from the news and reports of economic, behavioral, and environmental clues that storms across the globe are causing physical, mental, and financial stress on people. It is expected that mental stress will increase with challenges for worrying about making ends meet. However, your physical, mental, financial, and spiritual well-being is God's concern. He has made some recommendations in His words to guide and empower you to navigate every storm. The warnings about the effects of the storms, the reason for some storms and people's behaviors, the benefits of storms, and who is in those storms with you are outlined in His manual. God is in control of every creation to use timing, events, and storms to trigger people into actions to better their lives (Rom. 1:17). Some storms may be orchestrated by God to help us identify needs, breakdowns, shortcomings, and structural defects in both human and infrastructures.

You are properly equipped and linked to the Creator to handle every kind of storm. However, becoming unhappy with the very things He had created for your enjoyment can occur when you fail to reason with His seasons. Although most of us feel the pinch of the rising cost of living, unemployment, and other major losses, you should be mindful that there is always God's presence in every storm, and you should seek, find love, and trust Him, because God is love. Invariably, you should check around for His closeness in every storm. It may take a storm to bring that love inside of you out to melt the frozen river of joy for invention, bright ideas, patience, humility, and submission (Eph. 3:17–19). Experiencing various storms may be your opportunity to break the monotonous routine and do something different, like chatting with neighbors and getting to know total strangers who may be of use to you in the future. You are created to connect, relate, and reach out for others. A storm has a way of robbing you of your pride so that you seek help, even from those you would not talk to in normal circumstances. Some storms may offer you an opportunity to have a teachable heart. An unteachable heart is very prideful and rebellious, and it may not have respect for authority.

For those experiencing losses, it may be a good time to reorganize, retrain, re-engage, and embrace something new. Life comes with daily newness, and we should not hold tight to stale ideas. There is never a better time to encourage your children and loved ones to hope than during a storm. Some storms may be impactful enough to move those who refused to be moved because they were too comfortable. The effects of major storms are powerful enough to push everything in its path. In essence, experiencing a storm can become a transformer to love life again, refocusing, relearning, and listening to warnings in the future. The storm of life has a tendency to cause individuals to develop empathy for others who have faced likewise in their seasons (2 Tim. 2:24–26). It is not very wise to be provocative, snobbish, and judgmental to your associates, clients, and friends for not knowing the depth of their problems. Critics learn to refrain from being critical of others after encountering storms (Rom. 12:16). Thus, storms can become a melting pot used by God to teach people to be kind, broken, and loving in order to obtain favor and victory.

The storms of life may be God's way of giving you the opportunities to receive and give love. You are favored by God when you show love to people going through storms (1 Pet. 3:8–9). It is impossible to be broken for others when you are not broken by circumstances. Without storms and challenges, you may become too prideful, controlling, invisible, and drawn to the self, shutting others out of your life. You are created to be in relationships and to give and receive genuine love. For example, when you receive kindness from a total stranger after a flight's cancellation, having no way of getting home, you then realize the importance of others' kindness. The warmth of others by association, closeness and affiliation are sources that melt the ice of various storms of life. These storms come in multiple forms, like sicknesses, death of love ones, material and job loss, and physical and spiritual storms. We all need the warmth, support, and encouragement of friends and families to pull through the storms. Even though God is present in your storm, He uses people to bring relief. There is also the principle of giving to receive, and being involved in a friendship. There is never a better time to show love and kindness to others than when they are encountering storms. Love is the breaker of every storm. Being a neighbor's keeper is God's plan for all of us. The display of such is needed because each of us goes through the storm and needs each other's touch. This act of love may become an override to break the negative effects of the physical, mental, and financial stressors that storms may affect our various seasons (1 Cor. 13:4–8).

Your burden to reach out and touch others reinforces doing good to receive good things in return.

Taking Action to Effect Positive Changes in Your Environment for Your Own Good

Even though vital information to manage the ups and downs of life has been ingrained in every human, many platforms, educational materials, and social media are useful sources of information for insights on how to improve the quality of our lives with talents. Metrics of warnings, discernment of purpose, and finding ways to use our talents and maximize their capacity and scope to better our world is God's plan for each of us. However, it is up to the individual to realize his or her mission to impact the surrounding for return on investment. When the individual appreciates his or her value via education or by seeking information to make a difference in the lives of others, it then sets an environment of tackling problems in line with one's mission.

There are experts in many fields and with diverse skills to handle the changing needs of society. It is not a question of having the skills and talents required to care for the society, but the fear, doubts, timing, and commitment to go out to perform that plagues mankind. People are often focused with the past, uncertainties, and various changes in the economy and governmental structures to strategize. This kind of thinking affects our focus on what we can do to affect our surroundings, shifting it from what we can do to what is going in the environment.

Individuals are responsible for seeking the necessary support needed via choices of making plans to appreciate the values of others around them and then non-unilaterally affect the environment. Doing nothing or waiting for others to team up with you before taking important steps to make positive changes can put one into inaction. Your choice of friends, career, and spouse should be complementary. Supportive data and outcomes have established that those who take actions of warnings, symptoms, instruction, and information emerge as winners in whatever they do. Taking action is the fundamental point of life. Thus if you want to be enriched, fulfilled, productive, and involved, and be impacted to impact others, you must take action (Rev. 2:19). The focal issues of our world are embedded in dwindling economy, growing unemployment, inflation, healthcare issues, high school dropout, and more. Leaving these concerns to leaders and policy makers to seek best practices and to handle the myriad of issues is unreal. The fact of the matter is that we are all active contributors to whatever prevails in our environment. Your world is not meant to be for me, and you should not ignore the impact of your actions on others.

We are all gifted to discover, with implementation, ways and means to intervene, strategize, encourage, and complement each other. God does not have grandchildren, but He has children with gifts, intellect, and the ability to handle the world (Rom. 8:16). You are a perfect package and are well equipped to handle the world. Inferentially, we are struggling in this area for not successfully utilizing these gifts, given the results we are getting globally. How active are you in assessing what is not working in your immediate surroundings? If you are not happy about something, taking action to find the root cause is a great step for resolution. It is very easy to pinpoint problems at home, work, and throughout society. However, the best practice in solving any problem is taking action. It begins with an unbiased assessment that positions you to join others in solving problems for a better you. Every action and change begins with you. Action is your link to having your voice heard, to obtaining pertinent information and communication for desired outcomes. Until you act, you may never experience fulfillment. Your action is tangible evidence of putting your gifts to good use for joy and success (Eccles. 5:19).

The weight of your actions speaks volumes to draw people and even God's attention (1 Sam. 2:3) A person earnestly seeking employment will have a resume, go job hunting, and be ready for interviews. Staying home to think about having no job is an inactive behavior that has kept many people poor, jobless, and unfulfilled. God's words and promises are faith based, requiring actions to obtain your miracles. People may be puzzled by the action word, to act what you desire to get it (James 2:17–18). Hannah believed the words of Eli to change her appearance and utterances for positive results (1 Sam. 1:17–18). Your faith in action pleases God (Heb. 11:6). Faith is going into in action and believing in God's promises. Everyone has something to contribute to make a difference (1 Pet. 4:10). Sacrificial contribution is your love in action. This kind of sacrifice plays out in good parenting to nurture, protect, and ensure that the children realize their potentials. Society could pursue and reach out for things desired via joint actions, raising our children well. Nonetheless, persistence and reaching out to attain are examples of faith in action, and that pleases God.

The lessons learned are that you should anticipate what you desire by taking actions to prepare. Indulging in self-pity will perpetuate the challenges for not reaching for support. Seeing yourself as a failure and hopeless, and reflecting in your actions, is the opposite of faith. A firm belief that you will be out of debt involves taking actions to negotiate and begin to pay off those debts. Similarly, to be successful requires making strides to attract others and God to support you. Your actions affect your life, and you must act and make contributions for your world to blossom again. You have it in your hands to give and to refrain from looking outward for others to solve problems all the time. You will be much happier, enriched, and fulfilled when you consider yourself as being a stakeholder of effecting change. Your world will be deprived of your valuable inputs, assets, and talents when you wait on others to provide a notch before you can do your part to change with the changes. It is also important to know that changes never stop, so be ready to take risks to improve on your character, be open-minded, and embrace other life changers of our world.

An impact driven person is able to operate in a cross-system, cross-function and cross- societal domain crucial for success.

Addressing Issues of Life as You Network with Others

Victorious living results from actively working out things and not letting things worked themselves out for you (Eccles. 5:19). Your life could become a freefall, being bumped and tossed around, when you lack pertinent support. Family members and friends can provide some support, but you could lose your footage in life for not making your way successful (Prov. 4:1–13). Every stage in life has divine supports to move you to the next level; no one moves to the next level without proper handover to another level of support (Prov. 24:5–6). The supports of family members, as well as educational, spiritual, and other meaningful affiliations, are very indispensable regarding how things could turn out for you in life. You will be attracted to whatever authority you respect, and vice versa. Your life could be missing something if you do not lean on these supports for valuable lessons on how to work things out (Judg. 16:4–20). God's orchestrated design to network can be semantically stated that you are in a net together with others to work out things for mutual benefit. Thus, it is no longer profitable for anyone in the net to think sectional, individualized, or segregated thoughts for personal migration. It is also clearly evident that life is not static. It may take tripping and falling on your part to pay closer attention to those aspects needing some work as you climb the ladder.

The fact of the matter is that you are created to work out things (Deut. 28:12). That which you need in life will not come to you when you fail to sow the proper seeds toward desired harvest. It begins with having a mental picture of what you desire to accomplish in life to benefit the network. This mental image then becomes an indelible imprint to move you to seek the needed supports. However, your scope and seed of faith are your catapults to step out of your familiar zone and to take risks for your next level. Your performance at every stage provides rating from others as they observe to pitch. Traditionally, people have the tendency to hold on to familiar supports of friends and families for too long. Your progressive working out of things does not suggest hurting, stepping, and falling out with people; it does not suggest emotional and functional detachment of your meaningful relationships. The encouraging words, advice, support, and prayers of others are too powerful to be ignored (Prov. 9:8–9). Frequent, damaging reports about you could slow your move to the next level.

Believe it or not, your port of entry and parents, surrogate and natural, were planned ahead by God (Exod. 1:2–10). People who try to detach themselves from their surroundings may lack supports. The secret of victorious living is having a closer look at what is not working, which will challenge you to create a change to benefit the network. You are in a net. Hatred and constant complaints of what is not working will only create holes in the net (Prov. 25:28; 26:20). A huge hole in the net from bickering could sink everyone; this may be the case when a few greedy people make decisions without considering the adverse effects on others. Everyone in the net is responsible for his or her success to benefit all (Josh. 1:8)—God's words wouldn't have stated that the workers are few and the work is plenty, if this was not the case (Matt. 9:37). Many people are out of work. It is very clear that the music tone of recent times is different and requires a new dancing step. The time calls for paying closer attention to everything around you. It may take losing something and global shortfalls for some to watch their step and look within for hidden treasures. Whatever may be the case, working out things calls for expanding your horizon, extending your hands to reach out, and branching out into other fields to meet the changing workforce.

In essence, life is about service. Acquiring knowledge in your field of choice is not a restriction but a boast for flexibility (Eph. 5:16). Any form of knowledge or a talent not utilized to serve others may limit your visibility, promotion, and finance. In retrospect, working out life for success entails using whatever you have at present, which are the combination of your skills and a good nature to serve. This combination is usually a stepping stone to the next level (1 Tim. 4:14). Some degree holders may be starving while some non-degree holders may be swimming in wealth for refusing to work their way up. Thus, for those seriously looking for jobs, putting reasonable, affordable, available, and convenient services to practice will provide the noticeable visibility via watchful eyes of others for the next level. Life gives us pain, suffering, and problems to enable us surrender to proper authorities and to seek support from God via others. Your surrender will help you to walk in honor and respect, and to attract and serve people well for wealth.

People are strong link in the success of any institution. Impacting those around you prevents the huge costs of weak links.

Analyzing Your Impact to Improve and to Give Your Best to Receive the Best

Impact assessment is important during challenging and critical times, to enable you to determine your level of growth or retardation. The training, discipline, core values, and experiences of an early childhood impact life tremendously. Busy schedules and lack of knowledge may prevent significant influencers from taking time to impact the assessment of home front experiences, schools of choice, and extracurricular activities. There seems to be an underestimation of what little children are capable of handling in terms of learning, intelligence, accommodation, and inquisitiveness. Children are known to hide in secret places to watch and listen to conversations, and to then rebel against people of influence for being hypocritical. Oftentimes, mentors and significant others may be looked upon as being ill-equipped to order others. Thus, being mindful of your actions and surroundings, in terms of tardiness, accountability, availability, trustworthiness, and use of encouraging words, are very important because of their impact. The positive impacts of others may be crucial in reducing the problems and challenges of our modern times. People tend to engage in non-productive arguments to disqualify (Eph. 4:22–29). Impact assessment of what you are feeding your children socially, nutritionally, and motivationally, as well as an adherence to rules, are important. Early childhood impact is necessary to initiate changes of character, direction, and reformation to benefit (Eph. 6:4).

God also uses crises like economic meltdown, employers' diplomacy actions, rebellious behaviors in our children, homelessness, imprisonment, and the like to give us second chances in life. Oftentimes the earlier upbringing or association has not impacted us positively and requires some kind of surrogate to perform the job. However, ignorance can be a stumbling block and prevent you from getting needed training. Education, training, and motivational supports are the key components, reforming lives in places like drug programs. Your failure to see God as giving you a second chance will leave you complaining, murmuring, and telling others not to extend their hands to be lifted from the valleys. God uses your valleys to teach valuable lessons, when you stay long enough to have a one-on-one encounter with your heavenly father (Ps. 32:8) David's valley equipped him to learn to use his slingshot. He practiced and tested his skills in the valley, thus building confidence in his relationship with God (1 Sam. 17:34–51). This was possible because he chose to stay long enough to be motivated and inspired, and he derived his vision to the next level. No one else can attain these defining moments but you. Your tests and the outcome testimonies are visible proof that you have jumped the lighter hurdles to then mount higher. It takes your personal effort and consensual participation to obtain these unique lessons for your territorial mapping. Traditionally, every successful entrepreneur monitors and uses trends and analytical data to stay in business, and so should you. The mindset of hope, the willingness to change, and your faith in God is important in this journey (Ps. 104).

Your trust in God impacts your life no matter what your physical location or present predicament is, because you will be free from all fears, condemnation, and judgmental aspects of others (Prov. 29:25–26). God's words, testimonies, and experiences of others are valuable sources of ongoing learning to better yourself. Prosperity, growth, and innovation come from your willingness to hear God's voice as your shepherd (Isa. 40:11). He even uses your past mistakes to map out a new area of operation, because He is interested in what you will become. Your corresponding response requires your earnest assessment of your association, habits, and results. Wouldn't it be reasonable to change things and people that are not contributing to your growth (1 Cor. 15:33)? God is very concerned about you and is bent on doing whatever it takes to make you succeed, if you allow Him (Ps. 8:3–4). He knows the awesome gifts hidden inside of you: the ability to use His words and the Holy Spirit to support you every time you feel inadequate, incapable, and unmotivated, and when you short-change your potential. Knowledge, skills, talents, and habits—having the burden to use these attributes comes from your inner will, which works in contrast with the flesh and is the angry, territorial, unforgiving side, a void of love that tears down achievements (1 Cor. 8:1). Chaos, suffering, and the inability to utilize and blend the resources God has provided in people to care for a particular society result when everyone is puffed up for being a guru in his or her field. God is not trying to deprive you of good life, but He wants to develop the discipline, love, and empathy you need to dream, act, and live big—without making them idols for your destruction.

The secret to a successful life begins with studying your environment for strategies for improvement.

Challenging Yourself to Face Changes Needed for Positive Impact

The wind of change is blowing across nations, businesses, and cities. Staying calm during these windy, unfolding events on earth is crucial; it enables you to engage your mind and to obtain the right perspective required for noble actions. Most battles are now fought with a mind for individuals to neglect and to seek information for protection. A person with a sound mind will strategize to deal with all situations. However, having a sound mind comes from obtaining a daily dose of God's words to keep your mind at peace each day; it comes by developing a relationship with the person who has the blueprints of life in His hands. There is a tremendous relief when you see God as a friend, guidance counselor, and your ruler. It will be a great consolation to know that God knows your name and your parents' names even before you were born (Jer. 1:5) No human being has knowledge of that information, let alone or God's plans for him or her. He created all things, and His existence is endless (Heb. 7:16).

God does not change like the wind, seasons, economy, and people (Ps. 102:26). The most trustworthy people can say things they do not mean; they say things that you want to hear, to avoid offending you. People say wrong things because they do not know better. But God can never say things He does not mean. His plans, purposes, and love for you stay forever. It is your responsibility to change your attitude, believe in His promises, and face the winds of change around you. Changes are a must because things are not meant to stay the same. Thus, it is imperative that you study changes in people, situations, and the environment to make a noble impact. People are created to drive the changes as God's ambassadors on earth. He has also established in His words His desire for you to ask Him for the wisdom to embrace and use changes allowed by Him to bring improvement. God can never change for you. The daily reading of His words, and the application of them, will reduce fears, weaknesses, ignorance, hopelessness, and twisted thoughts, guiding you in all storms, hard times, and other dangers.

Your relationship with Christ, the Pathfinder, is important because He knows your career path. A little whisper of idea by Him in the guise of the Holy Spirit will solve phenomenal problems of the century. Joseph received such whispers to solve the food crises of the world (Gen. 41). He will provide you the wisdom to dig new oil wells when the old ones become dry (John 10:27); He whispers ideas of new technology to people that hang around Him(Ps. 23). People are suffering today because they are not hearing God urging them to shift gears, disconnect, and reconnect as needed. These factors may have contributed to winds of unrest, moral decay, microwave mentality, and rapidly evolving technology. There will be panic for those lacking God's directions of what He wants them to do. However, unknown is the fact that we are not fighting against physical things, but other factors that only His relationship reveals (Eph. 6:12).

God will not change to get you to buy His good plans. You are the one that has to change and align with Him. This is where it takes most people years to realize His good plans, after many mistakes. It is also possible that most people are living this life without knowing why they are here, let alone accomplishing divine purposes. If a driving license cannot be given to someone who can't read the signs or drive, how come people expect God to approve someone that is not ready to accept an assignment? This is the part that people neglect when they blame God during the delay period. Your change of heart to really relate to a God who made you for a noble purpose and with your interests at heart will definitely change your perspective to hear Him out by reading His manual for ideas, benefits, and hidden traps that have derailed many people. Without this relationship, you may be walking this life totally confused about what you are made of and where you are going.

A lot of people are very busy doing things that are totally different from what they are called here to do. It is quite obvious that we all have our own will. There is no willpower without a will. Even our Lord Jesus Christ had his will (John 5:30), but He submitted to the will of God to accomplish the very purpose of redeeming the entire world from the curses pronounced by God when Adam rebelled (Gen. 3:17–19). Salvation is your first step to walking in light again and recapturing those lost years of futility. Salvation comes through a personal relationship with Jesus Christ, the wind of hope in our windy world. Salvation provides you with the hope that your future is in His hands, whereby no other wind will blow you away (John 10–27). Salvation delivers you from guilt and lets you stand tall because of the freedom you now have to explore, obtain vision, and have revelations of the future like Joseph. There is no exclusion criteria to dreaming big and becoming a celebrity, even in a foreign land, when you embrace God's words and apply them to your life. It open doors of opportunities for you, having been given the keys to unlock new doors and lock old ones(Matt. 16:19).

Salvation has the soothing effect of giving you peace in times of stress, uncertainty, starvation, and frustration because your relationship with Him provides positive energy (Phil. 4:11–13). The daily life storms and their annoying problems will never cease. Societal issues, family problems, and massive layoffs are facts of life, and so are worries about how you will fit in into the big picture without Christ. The reciprocal effect of the microwave age, increased technology, and poor economy can limit opportunities to maximize the self. However, the hope in His assurance of salvation establishes that no trial, whirlwind, crushing wind, or storm will prevent you from living a victorious life. Your determination to get to know, talk to, and be ready to concern yourself with His interest will surely provide you with a firsthand experience of this faithful friend(Ps. 34:8). The story of how a person can be transformed from being an ignorant, laid back person to a wealthy, wise, father of faith was the beautiful story of Abraham, and this was possible because of his walk with God. The relationship took him places, putting him in situations to get rid of fears, prayerlessness, and disobedience, making him into an obedient, patient, wealthy man of prayer that interceded for others. Hence the lessons of life are taught and learned from various winds, storms, and unpleasant situations, which your obedience to His words provides. However, it takes making the Lord the ruler of your life to understand and learn these profitable lessons of life in order to prosper, making an impact as you travel (Gen. 12, 18).

You are a channel of change to change what is not productive to change others.

Changing With Changes, to Stay on Top as a Thriver

The changing trend in the climate, economy, and geopolitical and social environments could create some dysfunctional behaviors. However, staying prepared, committed, and focused have proven to be cost effective, productive, and fulfilling for individuals using protective guides to work their lives. It is always a challenge to build any structure like a home, business, organization—and even society because of the evolving myriad of players. For any of this entity to thrive without Godly principles (Ps. 127), each of the structures mentioned above will not succeed without the collaborative efforts of the people involved. On the contrary, collaboration is needed to unite the fronts and may tend to dwindle in crisis, poor economy, rumors of natural disaster, and hardship because of fear, panic, and misinformation. This is because any kind of loss and temporal displacement from homes or jobs creates frustration, panic, and doubts. However, it is expected to thrive, and we are all made to not shrink from using what we have at present to improvise and do well (2 Thess. 3:19). Naturally, hostility and intolerance are expected to rise when people face uncertainties at home and places of employment have a diminished return on investment. Nonetheless, people who go the extra mile at home, school, and work, to help the situations from their heart, get God's attention to step in to show His supremacy(Matt. 5:41).

Jealousy, envy, gossip, complaining, and grumbling do arise when people face danger, disaster, and adverse changes (Prov. 16:28; Jer. 20:10; Jude 16). People tend to feel jealous of whoever they feel is benefiting, by their definition. Jealousy may lead to gossiping about the person or the situation, for non resolution of the status quo. The display of these behaviors clutters the mind, which may affect the culprit's rational thinking. Catastrophes and adverse situations have proven to be golden opportunities to birth noble ideas and to bring every change to your favor (Prov. 8:12). Thus, thriving people are usually those who embrace every change and use it to better themselves and to better others and their environment. There is much to be gained in harnessing available resources and ideas, to pull each other up at home, work, and at the point of uncertainties, wants, and adverse situations. You are a superior being, unlike God's other creations, with the propensity to overcome barriers using everything life throws at you to learn, become well educated, and then educate others. The opposite behaviors are displayed by some people facing tough situations, whereby they create more stress, pain, and hardship to others (which is frowned upon by God) to get into deeper problems (1 Sam. 24: 1-7).

A person who thrives seeks improved exchange by not being influenced by what he or she sees or hears (Lam. 3:51). What you hear constantly can become internalized, if they are negatives, and it can affect and influence your thoughts. A thriver is not a time waster. Each second that passes can never be redeemed. Any wise individual should not engage in speculation and no action, when changes are taking place in the environment (Eph. 5:15–16). Have you realized that time wasters are usually bitter and angry for not applying their time wisely (Eph. 4:29–31)? Top performance thrivers are those who are very disciplined and are wise time managers, differentiating themselves from grumblers and shirkers. Those known as "shrinkers" shrink their resources and actions, doing well with scarcity and seeking revenge. Shrinkers only give out or give back to those who have given to them in the past, or to those likely to reciprocate—which is in contrast to God's words.

High performance thrivers are usually extra-mile individuals at home, school, and work and in any entity with creative ideas on how to improve services, reduce cost, and manage risks efficiently. They are the "What can we do to help?" kind of people. These people step up to use whatever is at hand to handle changes, challenges, and turbulences when others are busy regretting past actions, worrying about the future and listening to hearsay. High performance thrivers understand the Creator's flexibility, adaptability, and credenza of continuous improvement as an integral component of life. This lifestyle supports accountability, commitment, monitoring, tracking, and dealing with the present for understanding God's grace. Thrivers build on a strong foundation, which is Christ. They have insight that walking on the fast lane, building with the wrong material and location for great gain, may bring dishonor, discontentment, and failure. These individuals use God's words to build their lives to affect relationships, homes, businesses, and everything they touch for wealthy, healthy, and victorious life.

Front-liners are born leaders for choosing to trouble shoot issues others overlooked.

Confronting Issues Squarely for Impact

We all have things that bother us. This ranges from that nutty child making faces at you on the school bus, or that neighbor that complains about every slight noise. It may be that somebody in the office is making your life miserable. It may be that person who told you to your face that he or she will make sure that you will never get that grade to graduate, or that promotion, contract, or loan. There is nothing happening in the universe today that has not happened before. There is no issue faced by you today that someone else has not suffered in the past. The Israelites were confronted with this giant called Goliath, who was not only tormenting them for days with words but was also cursing God. His height, armor, and tone of voice put fear in everyone, including the armies (1 Sam. 17:23–50). No one was able to confront this giant until David—who understood the principle of the shield of faith and the sword of the spirit and the helmet of salvation—confronted him with God's words and killed him with just a slingshot. There are lots of things out there imaginary and real that your adversary uses to keep you from being who you are created to be. He uses people to create fear and hold you bound. People complain when they are faced with issues of life. God allows you to have these issues to develop confidence. Fear and intimidation come in various shades, color, size, and nature, and no one is immune to them. But it takes the word of God and your true relationship with Him to fight these (Col. 2:16). How can you keep records of your successes when you refuse to confront issues or certain people? We are yet to find out what goes through the mind of a pre-toddler before he or she takes that first step to learn to walk. The failure of a healthy child to walk at the right time becomes an early childhood intervention for the parents. In a nutshell, issues are inevitably planted here and there as obstacle courses to enable you to develop confidence, preparing you for the great future and to humble you to go to God for support.

Gigantic obstacles do surface in one's life and need to be confronted as one moves from one level to the other. These obstacles may be spiritually designated to require spiritual intervention from God for them to give in. This was the case with the Israelites and the Philistine giant named Goliath. The importance of fear in confronting the issues is displayed in this story for valuable lessons, for those on their way to make a huge impact. Thus, the inward fear in you has to be dealt with before you can deal with the fears others try to impose on you. David was able to defeat Goliath because he dispelled his own fear of using his bare hands to attack the lions and bears that came to attack his sheep. A lesson learned is to address every issue as it comes, to build your confidence. For example, allowing a little thing said or done to you to linger, simply because you are afraid to confront it, could pile up into a gigantic fear and become your personal Goliath.

What are you afraid of? What has someone in the past said to you that made you retreat into your shell and not come out? What have you seen or heard about the world and people that prevents you from exploring? It is very natural to run away from things and people that threaten you; no one is immune from threat. It is the way you confront your threats that makes you a winner. It is also your acceptance that threats are real challenges on which you need to work. A commander in chief of a great army may be afraid of cats. The lesson we learnt from the David and Goliath story is that it is very important to confront your fears. You must confront that very thing threatening your existence, not allowing you to sleep at night, and when you wake up in the morning, the same issue is there. No one can make meaningful headway with a Goliath challenging one's world. How many of you could function in a house badly infested with giant rats? You can't sleep, think, reason, or function because you are irritable, jumpy, and fearful.

The words of God have answers and solutions to confront every Goliath that threatens your life. God's words ask you to stand firm with the belt of truth. Even though no one is perfect, most of the things you are afraid of came from what you did or said, and they are avoidable when you walk in truth(Matt. 25:24–27). The watchful eyes of the Lord see you and will avenge you when you are lied to or when someone is sitting on your progress. The truth will prompt you to seek help when you are struggling with drinking or drug problems and other issues. There is a natural tendency to hide or cover up when you are confronted with issues. The lessons learned from people who have refused to confront these problems are loss of jobs, homes, or family members; incarcerations; and chronic diseases that result in untimely death. The truth is the word of God. David used these words of God to defeat Goliath. Most issues faced by many today are deeply rooted spiritual things that could be resolved through a relationship with God. Your body is craving for destructive things that could be very powerful and overwhelming. The tool available through His word lets you wear the breastplate of righteousness. Even in the carnal world, champions separate themselves from ordinary people; they do not act like everyday people on the street.

The teenage world is looking up to star football players as extraordinary people; society expects some code of conduct from them. A child of God is an extraordinary person and is expected to act and live right. You are a light as His child, and therefore you cannot hide among the crowd. As His child, you need to check yourself when you blend comfortably and unnoticed in a crowd. A child of God stands out and has godly charisma because of the character changes in him or her. A mind that thinks positive and think right will fear no accusation. You will have people's favors when God favors you. Honest living, respect, and love for others will liberate you from being afraid of things and negative consequences, because God stands for you (Phil. 4:8–9). Any offshoot of your old habit has to go in order to enable you live a liberated life.

An NBA basketball player knows what he will lose by not staying sober or engaging in things that will cause character assassination. Lots of us are living miserable lives because of our cynicism, corruption, selfishness, and sedentary lifestyle. You can walk in righteousness—it is in your DNA as a child of God. Righteousness is your ticket to defeating every Goliath that has bad influences over your children, stealing your health, joy, and possessions. You can get this righteousness through His word, which is also your defensive shield (Eph. 6:17), and it brings satisfaction. This satisfaction comes because you see yourself as an image of God being creative (Ps. 8:5–8). It makes you contribute because you have a positive image of yourself that God is behind you in all that you do.

Righteous people take chances and risks because of their visions. They are positive thinkers because they see themselves as God's gifts, and their ideas come from God. Unlike worldly opinions, righteous people are full of joy because they engage themselves, trying things to better their world. They may fail here and there, but their persistence enables them to build their self-esteem. Happiness, excitement, enthusiasm, and youthful exuberance follow righteous people; the words of God renew them. The words of God is also an offensive tool that wards off every Goliath in your path, when you use it at your disposal to overcome anger, bitterness, unprofitable habits, unproductive lifestyles, low self-esteem, and other things that keep you in bondage. Lastly, it is evidenced that David used his faith to conquer fear. Your faith will increase daily when you make time in your daily chores to read God's manual to obtain faith. You will not only receive more revelations of where and when your inputs are needed for impact, but also His supports will level the ground for you (Dan. 3:17).

Peace with love is the language of resolution in dealing with problematic individuals.

Developing an Endpoint Lifestyle to Embrace the Future

The evolving changes in the global economy have necessitated a call to reform the healthcare, financial, and housing markets. It is a cultural shift from being a spectator to a participator. The time of mediocrity is over for any competent adult to embrace a social environment whereby everything is done for the person. A participatory environment has been put into place by God right from the beginning. Participation does not only add value to life but brings character transformation to propel you from one level to another. There is happiness, victory, prosperity, and fulfillment in any environment, whereby all participants take active roles. God is a potter, an artist who packages and molds with purpose in mind (Jer. 1:5). God sees you from an endpoint of His design from the beginning (Jer. 29:11); this is the same way an artist sees the finished product in his or her mind's eye before the completed masterpiece. An artist already had a mapped out plan of his or her design before starting. The value of a masterpiece and targeted clients are also figured out before design. The material delay and third-party interference, including disappointment and criticisms, are factors that any committed artist ignores to stay focused (Hab. 2:3). The mental picture of the masterpiece is enough inspiration to not give up. You are created with mental capacity to envision the finished product in your mind in order to strategize on how to execute the plan step by step. An endpoint lifestyle is a life of faith that God has in mind for us all in order to be successful. Without this faith, it may be impossible to resist the temptations that derail your destiny. A person who is earnestly seeking to effect changes positively in the society must have faith to work out things, study the needs of others, and strategize with hope that his or her efforts, by God's grace, will produce the results.

An endpoint lifestyle is God's plan for mankind to move us from being sluggish, procrastinating, irresponsible, and unaccountable (Prov. 20:26). An idle life is never God's plan for anyone. The proof of your faith is evidenced in your works. Faith is very contagious and, as a result, produces outcomes that reach others. Thus, faith and endpoint lifestyle are similar. Endpoint lifestyle is a commitment driven to perform your tasks regardless of how those around you neglect their roles. Endpoint lifestyle is commitment that is driven, as in marriage. For any marriage to have a fruitful endpoint, there must be commitment to see godly visions for members of the family to hold on during challenging times. God painted a solid picture of staying committed as a driving force for every marriage, whereby He brings together two total strangers to become an instrument to bring His gifts to the world.

Children, the product of marital union, are God's way of introducing new talents and the workforce of the future. God finished all creation long time ago within seven days (Gen. 2:3). However, He uses the gifting in children to provide various talents needed to improve what was originally created (1 Pet. 4:10). Every raw material there is today was available thousands of years ago; however, God is always ahead of all modern technology, giving wisdom via unique talent to every individual to improve the earth. It is a quality force model to serve the world, meeting every need (Gen. 1:26–28). Replenishing the earth is a workforce model of using specialization and educational, industrial, spiritual, operational, and intellectual competencies to meet the various needs of society. It begins with initial indoctrination at home to establish those fundamental principles of life (Deut. 6:6–9). For example, being sluggish starts at home. Thus, training a child to not leave the last string of toilet paper for someone else to fill up is a good way to discourage being slothful, which God hates. Identifying areas of competence and specialization early at home is very effective in developing a future workforce (Ps. 101:2–7). The home front participation in identifying and growing the future workforce is God's plan for society; it is a model of an excellent guide to develop leaders, teachers, statesmen, and technicians at every operational level of the society. Thus, any neglect at the home front, on academic and technical competencies, will rob society of employment and technology. God's model to meet the needs of the world supports a team approach to use each other's strengths, ideas, weaknesses, mistakes, needs, failures, talents, and differences to build up each other and society.

The endpoint approach to develop self and society does not only bring industrial development but also the discipline and dedication to remain on the job. This is achievable when people take to heart the outcome of their actions in the future and refrain from doing certain things. A careful thought of the end result of robbing a bank, walking out of a job, walking away from your family, and drinking or eating what is known to affect your health, are examples of endpoint approaches to revitalize your life (Heb. 10:35–36). You are called to participate by building your home, workforce, and society and not destroying it. A participatory lifestyle is committal and communicative, with the involvement from an artist standpoint to produce a masterpiece. However, the design of a committed person with a derivative vision from God stands out (Jer. 23:15–16). God-driven designs come with resources, connectivity, burdens, love, patience, grace, and the character transformation to stay on top (2 Pet. 1:5–8). It is only a defiant person who will not know that God is calling the world into action on those neglected, basic life principles. It is not by coincidence that there are action words lately on wellness, healthcare, and financial and educational reforms. These buzzing words are signs to wake up and think about the endpoint, focusing on why you are here on earth. It is a revolutionary call to reassess your life for better health and a relationship with God and people. This thought is very provoking, exciting, and hopeful to get involved once more without pride and prejudice for a wealthy you and an improved society.

Your future is determined by your ability to reform those unprofitable habits retarding your growth.

Embracing Challenges as a Gateway for Impact in Order to Prosper

Challenges have resurfaced here and there to affect the economy at large. Nonetheless, challenges have known to motivate people to become innovative and creative as they search for solutions to problems. Going extra miles, taking risks, and seeking pertinent information are also expected in order to increase oneself during challenging times. I am convinced that people who ordinarily will not look for alternatives to protect their jobs will move with new trends, take risks, and be forced to do so during crunch times (Eccles. 3:1–8). Many businesses are finding alternative ways to trim the fat, resorting to better revenue cycles, bulk purchases, and having some kind of merger. As imaginary as it may seem, the collection of many drops of sweat from a group of people determined to find solutions can form a dam to generate electricity from trying (Eccles. 4:9). Thus, challenges can become a propelling force to creating better networks, accountability, and down-sizing for personal, professional, and institutional growth. Thus, facing challenges should be seen as a gateway to make better use of things in us that we did not think was there; to not despair but instead have hope when facing challenges.

Challenges are triggers to target actual domains, areas of impact, and needs with careful planning. Challenges are also enablers to move individuals to maximize themselves, reduce waste, practice time management, and become creative in running their lives and businesses. In retrospect, meeting needs and dealing with challenges and problems are few reasons for seeking knowledge. However, the missing part is that God gives people the ability to make wealth (Deut. 8:18). Knowledge is powerful in bringing your plans to fruition; the seedling to solve problems is inside each individual to progress in life no matter the situation. But it is left for individuals to discover, nurture, and use their seeds to make a noble impact (Ps. 32:8). The mind has to be challenged by need, threat, or burden to actually figure out what to do as the need arises. An unchallenged person will do nothing but complain, criticize, or manipulate in order to be provided for. The real knowledge to break through in this life comes from God's words. A whisper of God's words can change the economy of a nation (Gen. 40:33–40). A receptive and renewed mind will program and reprogram us to handle issues of life as they unfold with hope, peace, and faith (Isa. 40:31).

It is from God's manual that you will discover that you are gifted to be motivated to use them and to embrace reforms (Eccles. 5:19). Reforms are usually triggered by needs and challenges; it may never occur to certain people that they have specialized talents until people are pushed to the tight corner with nowhere else to go, and then they'll look within. Our world will always go through various climatic, economical, structural, and physical changes. However, we are responsible for prioritizing and managing time and resources. It is obvious that having plenty on one's plate can become a deterrent to develop skills, patience, and character needed to impact others for seeing no need to look for alternatives or face the problems of our world.

The Creator has already given you a mandate to increase, multiply, and impact your environment (Gen. 9:1–7). You cannot prosper without planting your seeds to reap the harvest. Your expectation of your environment will be the driving force to devote time for its improvement. Your scope and the extent you are willing to go will also determine the level of influence. You will obtain enough for yourself and your immediate family, if you focus on such. People who are limited in their dreams may not see the need to reach out. Expanding your horizon expands your knowledge, experience, and the ability to face life in general. Innovators, inventors, and the majority of people making a difference are those who recognize that wellness and wealth are dependent on their positive impact to society at large (Gal. 6:9). Challenges and scarce resources are motivators to do just that to prosper.

In retrospect, your area of impact unfolds when you discover your purpose via God's words. The more you seek this knowledge, the more revelation you obtain to navigate your world successfully. There are so many issues to be tackled, just as there are so many people to handle them. The non-transfer of noble ideas, talents, character, and certain skills and technology will result in importing them from others at a higher cost, and it may be of lesser quality. This is the result of a lack of positive impact as food for thought. Reformers, mavericks, and influential people are those who understand the importance of positive impact in developing great minds and society at large.

Transformation for reformation is achieved when members see each other as co-contributors to respect and build up for contributions.

Engaging People around You to Succeed

Engaging people around you to do something meaningful has never been more paramount in our lifetime than at the very present. It is becoming harder and harder to get anyone to do something meaningful, even for his or her well-being. Even the very laws to guide us are taken advantage by people who do not know that there is value, joy, and pride in engagement. It may sound ridiculous, but human nature has a way of creating walls, boundaries, and beneficial information blocks. Most of us have managed to do some patches, overlooking certain things to get by structures and resistance because of their understanding of the benefits. If you have lived long enough or have children and are married, you will testify that it is more peaceful to work around some situations in order to avoid conflicts and confusion. This article takes a critical look at how life will be made easy when each and every one of us stays committed, open-minded, responsible, accessible, flexible, and willing to put down our hats for others, with better suggestions and skills for mutual benefits.

Creating unnecessary social, professional, gender, or even age-related barriers can sometimes hinder one's predisposition to welcome valuable ideas. There are varying issues in our lives that are attributed to physical and physiological stages of one's life. However, most of the issues associated with these can be dealt with, especially when they are known to prevent the culprit from engaging the self for success.

The dilemma of life may begin with being born and raised in an impoverished, violent, non-trusting environment, where survival of the fittest dictates the pace. There is no way an unsupportive environment could not affect one's character, even at the onset. Nonetheless, there are useful and healthy information exchanges, with God's words to rebuild your life. It is very clear that there are obstacles in everybody's path, however the knowledge that you will always emerge a winner per God's words to follow the path He has preordained for you to navigate against any obstacle is sure a soothing feeling. It is hard to engage anyone who is used to hearing the negatives or being told that he will not amount to anything without the help of God's words. Even when you think you have it made, the uncertainties of what could be and the vying eyes of others are enough to create fear. This is where faith exists in all of us. Faith can only be acquired from hearing God's words. Fear is the opposite of faith, acquired from the absence of knowing the will, benefits, and God's protection to panic all the time.

Faith teaches that you can joyfully do anything for having received Christ, who has cancelled the power of fear to live victoriously (Heb. 2:14–17). All our suffering resulted from separating ourselves from the very one that has life, blessing, health, prosperity, wisdom, and harvest via Adam and Eve. Doubters may comment, "Why didn't God foreknow that this bridge would take place?" The answer is how responsible, committed, and matured you can be to engage yourself when everything is done for you. For those having plans to go somewhere, it usually takes a mistake to not miss it again. You were created to have better relationships with others, starting with God. Without God and His meaningful words in your life, it is almost impossible to engage yourself, let alone others.

The lack of discipline can crash the very empire, relationship and even the society you have worked so hard to build.

Everyday Secrets to Working Your Way to Succeed

Victorious living results from working out things and not letting them work themselves out for you (Eccles. 5:19). Your life could become a freefall from being bumped and tossed around, when you lack pertinent support. Family and friends could provide some support, but you could lose your footage in life for not making your way successfully (Prov. 4:1–13). Every stage in life has divine support to move you to the next level; No one moves to the next level without a proper handover to another level of support (Prove. 24:5–6). The supports of family members, as well as educational, spiritual, and other meaningful affiliations, are very indispensable as to how things could turn out for you in life. You will be attracted to whatever authority you respect to move toward them, and vice versa. Your life could be missing something by resorting to not leaning on these supports for valuable lessons on how to work out things (Judg. 16:4–20). God's orchestrated design to network can be semantically stated that you are in a net together with others, to work out things for mutual benefits. Thus it is no longer profitable for anyone in the net to think sectional, individualized, or segregated thought for personal migration. It is also clearly evident that life is not static; it may take tripping and falling on your part to pay closer attention to those rotted woods needing some work as you climb the ladder.

The fact of the matter is that you are created to work out things (Deut. 28:12). Things you need in life will not come to you when you fail to sow the proper seeds toward the desired harvest. It begins with having a mental picture of what you desire to accomplish in life to benefit the network.

This mental image then becomes an indelible imprint to move you to seek the needed supports. However, your scope and the seed of faith are your catapults to step out of your familiar zone and to take risks for your next level. Your performance at every stage provides rating from others as they observe to pitch in words for you. Traditionally, people have a tendency to hold on to familiar supports of friends and families for too long. Your progressive working out of things does not suggest hurting, stepping, and falling out with people; it does not suggest emotional and functional detachment of your meaningful relationships. The encouraging words, advice, support, and prayers of others from birth to the present are too powerful to ignore (Prov. 9:8–9). Frequent damaging reports about you could slow your move to the next level.

Believe it or not, your port of entry and parents, both surrogate and natural, were planned ahead by God (Exod. 1:2–10). People who try to detach themselves from their surroundings may lack supports. The secret of victorious living is having a closer look at what is not working to challenge you to create a change in order to benefit the network. Hatred and constant complaints of what is not working will only create holes in the net (Prov. 25:28; 26:20); a huge hole in the net from bickering could sink everyone in the net. This may be the case when a few greedy people make decisions without considering adverse effects on others. Everyone in the net is responsible for his or her success, to benefit all (Josh. 1:8). God's words wouldn't have stated that the workers are few and the work is plenty, if this was not the case (Matt. 9:37). Many people are out of work; it is very clear that the music tone of recent times is different and requires a new dance step. The time calls for paying closer attention to everything around you. It may take losing something for some people to watch their steps, and the global shortfalls for some to look within for hidden treasures. Whatever may be the case, working out things calls for expanding your horizon, extending your hands to reach out, and branching out into other fields to meet the changing workforce.

In essence, life is about service. Acquiring knowledge in your field of choice is not a restriction but a boast for flexibility (Eph. 5:16). Any form of knowledge and talent that is un-utilized in serving others may limit your visibility, promotion, and finance. In retrospect, working out life for success entails using whatever you have at present, which is the combination of your skills and good nature to serve. This combination is usually a stepping stone to the next level (1 Tim. 4:14). Some degree holders may be starving while some non-degree holders may be swimming in wealth and refusing to work their way up. Thus, for those seriously looking for jobs, putting your reasonable, affordable, available, and convenient services to practice will provide the noticeable visibility via watchful eyes of others for your next level. Life gives us pain, suffering, and problems to enable us surrender, to proper authorities, and to seek supports from God via others. Your surrender will help you to walk in honor and respect to attract and serve people well for wealth.

A balance life is a balanced act of discipling self to eat, think, act, visualize and impact others as you function in your disciplines.

Getting the Right Reception Link
Necessary for Impact

The ability to receive clear audio and visual for television, radio, and IT networks is dependent on proper linkage to satellite and bandwidth receptors. Gone are the days when aluminum foil and coat hangers are used by those who cannot afford TV antennas. Your mind is a free gift information jack for the rest of the body; it is your God-given linkage for motivation, restoration, virtualization, creativity, and repentance. It is your memory chip with a daily upgrade, an update with a virus protection, when you take time to study God's words daily. You pick up historic, analytical, benchmarking, and highly intelligent information from God's words in order to navigate this word. A lack of this link brings loneliness even with money, a successful career, and people around you.

You receive a code alert of impending danger when you listen to the still, small voice inside of you. Mother hen has a way of picking up the vibration that a hawk is close by, and she can warn young chicks to take cover. Ants have built-in sensors to know when an adverse season is approaching to store up food (Prov. 30:25–28). God equips nature, little creatures, and inanimate objects with survival kits to detect issues and fend for themselves. You are not left alone to parade the earth without a link to same information command center. Those who believe in God and His words tap into the built-in antenna to study, analyze, and operate within its guidelines, taking actions to navigate successfully (Dan. 11:32). Do you ever study some repeatable things in your world for trending, planning, correcting, and directing? You have an inward visualization to operate on multiple frequencies, unlike other creatures (1 John 4:4). The authority comes by proper linkage with God. A lot of people are stagnated by not tapping into their spiritual antenna to visualize, attain, and plan for rainy days. You will be reduced into a fleshy, reckless consumer without focus, planning, work ethic, security, and spiritual maturity (Ps. 32:8).

The hard drive of a computer is its main frame. Your mind is the main frame link to your conscience that speaks clearer as the Holy Spirit, when you accept Christ as your savior. The new link advances you to pursue profitable ventures (2 Kings 7:1–18) and acts as a restraint to discipline you to make good choices. Without it, you can become so much involved in your relationships, career, and geographical locations that you come to the end of the rope still feeling empty. The link prompts you to see God's words as a data governance and management tool, to inform you that there is no entrapment, closed doors, lost hope, and derailment for a person who knows God (Prov. 3:13–26). This knowledge enables you to avoid costly mistakes and to walk your way back to recovery after a major loss (Luke 15). It will help you to avoid duplication and to visualize without missing your target. King David had his spiritual antenna plugged in to discern that the battle with Goliath was won already; he did not waste his time wearing the heavy armor and using a sword (1 Sam. 17:22–51). He would have failed had he duplicated what the commanding officers did, to no avail (1 Cor. 2:3–5). Rather, he used his link to reach out for a bandwidth wave of heaven for a high-speed frequency laser. Most of us have strained and stressed in life for not connecting to God's powerful link. It is obvious that a stubborn chick who ignores the danger signal of the mother hen will become prey for a hungry hawk (Ps. 91:1–7).

The most valuable lessons in life are those learned from close calls and nearly negative experiences. People who desire remakes use these valuable lessons to improve, avoid risks, and acquire wisdom. Most close calls may be a way of telling you to be very careful, slow down, watch, and trace back steps to that particular place or time when you think you have lost something and need to recover it (Jer. 29:11). However, it takes a thought-provoking person with godly linkage to humbly do a self-assessment of every asset loss and every professional, physical, and social decline. Anyone can lose money, a career, respect, relationships, and a business due to poor management, but a remake can correct it. It takes just one silly mistake for a highly intelligent, successful person to experience ruin to the point of devastation. Even at that point, the Holy Spirit is your antenna to link you again after your repentance. Your obedience to God's words enables you to discern danger and make a contract for safety, to see golden opportunities in rejected ventures, and to toughen you up in every crises so that you emerge victorious in the long run (Job 23:10). It is un-wise to miss this multi-source depot with collaborative heaven linkage, providing you with quality decisions, high performance, and the analytical intelligence to refrain, delve in, divert, and contract for safety. It is through God's words that you can distinguish between other interfering, buzzing signals (Prov. 8:12). Your spiritual antenna will remain high when you operate with historical data, benchmarking, and the futuristic information that God's manual provides (Deut. 8:18).

Your capabilities to handle life is re-charged daily by lessons, experiences and signals received to embrace our highly complex environment.

How to Obtain High-Intelligence Informatics for Vision and Impact

Traditionally, present outcomes result from the plans of the past to ignore the importance of high-intelligence information, for strategic operational planning. The complexity and rapid changes of our world economically and technologically with informed consumers, poses even greater challenges for traditional planning. The result of any plan is as good as the quality, timeliness, scope, and functionality in meeting the needs of people. Thus the success of an individual, business, profession, or entity is dependent upon obtaining the right information in a timely manner for planning, resource allocation, and trends to make quality decisions. Targeted vision, focus, and ability to identify the changing needs of people and society makes any first responder a visionary. The reality of life is that your success story begins and ends with people to direct your whole life, looking for ways and means to make a difference in alignment with God's will. Usually late responders miss the royalty and get leftovers. You are created with an originality, to come up with bright ideas for unique impact, when you uncover your purpose.

The story of Esau and Jacob is a very good narrative of how things can shift from being a lead person to being led. Jacob was the first responder and quenched the immediate hunger of his father Isaac, to receive all the blessings by God's timing (Gen. 27). Esau was superficial, fleshy, uncalculated, and careless about Godly ideas for his purpose (Gen. 25:29–34). Esau thought it was business as usual and went about his business without seeking God's direction: to work so hard to please his earthly father. Little did he know that God provides for those who seek Him to impact their world and receiving blessings. Thus without God's words, you will be self-limited to know His plans for you, which may lead you to work unnecessarily harder than others.

You are created to make an impact using ideas and thoughts whispered by the Holy Spirit. Material things cannot drive destiny, however an idea, information, and noble thought can transform a poor person, society, and a nation into wealth. In retrospect, a person may lack divine ideas for being very superficial with a narrow focus, self-limited for not knowing how to use the raw materials that are intertwined in one's purpose. A superficial person is negligent about spiritual things, the engine driver of God's purpose (Matt. 6:33). Discerning God's purpose in one's life and pursuing it brings wealth, health, peace, and joy, making one an overflow for others.

Esau was the first son of Isaac, making him the benefactor of his father's inheritance. However, his failure to discern the significance of his position and purpose put him in harm's way. The blessing of Isaac was attached to birthing the nation of Israel. Esau missed this by not having an idea of what was deposited inside of him to give it up. Most of us are doing the same thing by not seeing the big dream and purpose in our lives, children, and society. There is greatness in all of us, but you have to see it. The craving for that high-intelligence information to derive vision and purpose is inert in you; the quest for information is part of mankind. However, a lack of understanding and disrespect for divine and earthly authority may prevent people from submitting themselves to obtain vital information. There are so many complex and external infringements to not lean on the Creator, the giver of visions (Ps. 121). He knows the world, the people in it, and your assignment so well that leaning on Him makes your life easy and prosperous. His guidelines do not inflict pain, fear, and limitations, but he has cautions here and there with speed bumps to put you back on track. You need God's words to have profitable ideas on how to multiply, replenish the earth, promote health, and protect yourself.

The lesson learned from Esau's story is that we are ill equipped to handle divine purpose without divine intervention. The discernment of Rebecca provided Jacob with the visibility, simplification, monitoring, and troubleshooting that made his life prosperous. This high intelligence is found in God's words, which explain the principles of empathy, kindness, humility, and putting God in the midst of everything you do to succeed. Without God's words, you will be self-limited and narrow-minded, and you will put God on the back burner to receive only what is there for you, a food for thought like Esau. God is not looking for perfection, but the obedience and willingness to make a U-turn when convicted. Operating in one's divine destiny provides peace, blessings, protection, wealth, and satiation for doing the will of the Almighty God (Ps. 37:37) In a nutshell, you are created to fulfill a purpose: to become rich in every aspect. However, your life will be simplified and successful when you use trends and guidelines from God's words to mirror your life and impact your environment (Heb. 4:12).

Associating with informed and refined people enables you to acquire qualifying behaviors, to embrace changes to function in your defined territories.

Impacting Lives by Encouraging Independence

Enabling others to depend on you for control and mastery, and to earn respect, has its cost on society. You may be enabling others to depend on you when you fail to provide the knowledge and help they need to stand on their own feet. Your negligence in assigning or delegating tasks and responsibilities to your children and staff members could rob them from earning valuable experiences needed to navigate life successfully. People who have difficulty trusting others may decide to do everything at home or on the job to deprive others of the necessary exposures and skills needed to be independent (Col. 3:23–25). Independence enables one to take risks and experience life as it is, a mixture of good and bad, ups and downs, highs and lows. A person isolated to any of these extremes may have a problem facing challenges. There is also tendency for individuals who do not know how to face challenges to give up very easily, which affects one's ability to live a purposeful life. Everybody is created by God to do something in life. Everyone has been given talents for meaningful use in order to impact the lives of others. Any environment that suppresses this progression toward independence creates un-fulfillment.

Life is complex, affected by cultural environment and some beliefs, habits, values, and principles to ignore God, who knows the beginning and the end (Ps. 94:9; 32:8). Embedded in life are parental dispositions and socially acquired ways of thinking that may affect independence. God expects everyone to grow daily using learned and acquired behaviors to gain independence. God's words provide leverage to parents, leaders, and mentors to influence people in their paths to become independent. A home is an important starting point to build a strong society for children to adopt and emulate what they see at home (1 Chron. 12:32). It is very hard to walk your way back and reestablish independence once it has taken root in someone else. There are certain things timing could not bring back, warranting an early start to teach children to accept responsibility (Eccles. 3:1–8).

How could you expect someone who has never handled chores at home to learn some skills and be responsible for others? It is to the benefit of a person to disconnect from people who do not know how to delegate responsibilities and who lack time management. Time is given to us all to develop our talents and to build our life to achieve goals and purpose. God is a father who knows the ruins of dependency to establish roles, commitment, trust, valuable principles, input and output, and chains of command (Ezek. 44:4–5). Comforts, non-productivity, non-participation, challenges, and responsibilities are not God's plans for people. God values your participation and using your talents to bring the best when you submit. He will use what you love and hate to engage you to be victorious. The same participation is expected of all people to wean off those under their authority from comforts and a laid-back mentality.

Building your life upon the platforms of others and material things cannot provide fulfillment (Isa. 40:28). It is like building your life on a platform outside God's plans for you. God's platform provides wisdom, mappings, visualization, and inward strength to gain control of your domain. He gave you the assigned areas of influence with supported features, skills, and network connections. Jesus Christ is the light of people—your vision comes from Him (Isa. 42:6). He is the strength to the poor and the needy; He is your strength in all your weaknesses. We are helpless without God. People and things we are dependent upon will never uplift us or enable us to overcome our weaknesses. The realization that you are helpless without Him is your surrender in having your needs met (Isa. 25:4). He is a sure foundation, making every other manmade foundation a shadow to those within (Isa. 28:16).

You need the light of God in your life to live and see your way out of darkness (Isa, 60:20). He is your guiding light in this turbulent world; you never worry about unfolding events when you trust God. Jesus Christ has open arms so that you can receive His light, which comes with showing you the secret weapons to prevent loss of vision and dominion. His light provides best practices to obtain and manage your resources very well. It educates you to avoid mistakes of life that retard your progression. It prevents catastrophic experiences that come from not listening to the warnings of the Spirit of God in you. Your trust in God is a proactive step for provision, security, direction, and interactive life learning to positively impact your championship walk.

Friends and family members may offer help in a crisis, but be mindful that you are a replica of God, created to live by principles with shared loss risks and benefits. He has numbered the strands of your hairs, and you should depend on Him for your audience-specific mapping. How can you reach this group God has mapped out for you when you are dependent on things, substances, and people to feel good? Enabling others to remain dormant and unfulfilled has a sharable effect on us all. Helping each other kick those habits that are making us unproductive becomes the responsibility of all of us, as we contain cost and provide employment for a better future. It is imperative that individuals whose cultures disproportionately assign tasks to some gender, to affect their learning and commitment, reconsider the impact and make amends.

The global economic meltdown, advent in technology and job scarcity are examples of phenomenal changes that may linger on for a while, for everyone to renew the way they have looked at things in the past and change certain habits. With high cost of living, reduced benefits by employers, and program cuts, it is imperative that individuals expand their horizon, watching the needs of their environment to develop programs and pertinent shifts in technology needed to accommodate the crossroads; this requires the corporation of everyone to move forward. While resistant to change is common among those wanting to remain due to the fear of changing the status quo, the culprits should also be aware that they may make others dependent on them, which obstructs progress. Becoming independent enables individuals to cross a road without the undue stress and anxiety that depending on others brings.

Failure to warn, encourage or mentor may silence crucial voices of the future reformers and mavericks.

Inspiring Others by Becoming Appreciative

Pride, arrogance, and a lack of knowledge may prevent some individuals from appreciating the friends, mentors, professionals, and noble influencers that have sustained all of us to date. Could you imagine what your situation would be without various professionals in every field making our lives easier? These people may have influenced you or touched your life to hope, be who you are, and maintain the state of health you are in today. Even the most wealthy, talented, beautiful, and influential people must have had individuals who saw such potential in them and encouraged them to climb higher. Verbal appreciation, little chances to try out things, and every opportunity given to you to engage in new ventures have a huge tendency to boost your self-esteem, which is needed to develop your vision. People and society perish where there is no vision (Prov. 29:18). Your horizon will be broadened to begin to see visions of greatness, victory, and achievement as you see a significant personality in your life engage in things some may have thought were impossible.

This is your season to reflect on those situations, individuals, and opportunities that you may have thought were horrific but that have helped shaped your perspectives about life to become whom you are. People sometimes believe those who challenge them into noble action are harsh. Joy, happiness, fulfillment, and the will to live come from the feeling that one has achieved something in life. These all stem from parents, influencers, mentors, friends, bosses, teachers, encouragers, and professionals. Be grateful, for what would we have been without them?

You should be thankful for special abilities that you have been taken for granted. People are encountering problems by not realizing that they are unique and to not let others define them. Many people are working poor and are miserable because they're not recognizing the gifts and visions God has given them (Exod. 36:1–2). God has the mission statement for everyone that matches the gifts and talents. The work and walk of anyone who sticks to this mission statement to derive his or her vision testament will experience a jointly fitted, step-by-step, illuminated path to stardom (1 Tim. 6:16). The person will enjoy the best fruits of his or her efforts for plucking them from the tree of life, which is God's word. The person will reflect God's goodness and glory for displaying abundance, joy, and thankfulness, partnering with God and being waited on by the angels all the time (Heb. 1:13–14). God's mission statement for each individual comes with a package for health and vision, enabling one to perform with unique features, limitations, and provisions. Each of us is provided with a tunnel vision to see our tools and mappings, which may appear meaningless for others. Beam with gratitude for the almighty God, whose throne is in heaven, and the earth His footstool (Isa. 66:1).

You will never mature when you are cushioned from pain, adversity, and mistakes. Pain can be a good eye-opener to move the opposite direction; it is a learning mechanism to accept things not planned for and to avoid a big crash from little issues. As gruesome as it may seem, mistakes are good, and we should be thankful for them. You have to miss what you probably had in mind, examine it to determine that it wasn't your take, and then go back and not miss it again. Mistakes also give you the opportunity to go to God for renewal of strength. You need His awesome power to unveil your dreams, ideas, and talents as you travel to better your world (Isa. 40:30–31). Further, issues in life have their ways of causing sufferers to be humble, tolerant, and compassionate of others. Understanding your purpose in this life is very important for satisfaction, unlike earthly possessions. The only way to find this purpose is by partnering with God clothed in majesty, power, honor, and light to change your outlook, and to also feed you the best food for longevity, prosperity, wealth, and health (Deut. 28:1–14).

The rain, sun, dew, and wind can never be bought by anyone, no matter how wealthy. The very least items have been provided free of charge so that you do not have to wake up every morning thanking the Creator and the giver of various talents in people to provide goods and services to you. Your thankful act begins with praying to hear God's heartbeat for you, in order for your heart to beat for others (Jer. 33:3; 1 Tim. 2:1).

Good friends are treasures. God is greater than all the good friends in the universe put together. Act wisely by honoring God as a faithful friend to thank, acknowledge, and appreciate in season and out of season, so that you may be seasoned to prosper (2 Cor. 8:9).

Appreciating the value of people and things around you appreciates their values.

Lack of Knowledge Will Enlist Your Name in the Hall of Failure

Lack of knowledge regarding your right to prominence, authority, opportunities, access, bargaining power, and safety nets are reason for failing in life. Any information blockage, regardless of source, is robbing you of progress toward your purposeful mission on earth. You have been charged to take care of all living and nonliving things around you. Obedient living things have enhanced sensitivity to operate in the environment with other hosts. We may have lost that sensitivity when Adam and Eve hardened their hearts via disobedience (Gen. 3:17–19). The historical fact is that all human minds are as hard to read for not reading the blueprint of life (the Bible) for their renewal. An inert sensitivity provides information, operational framework, trends, habitat, and contract for safety by the Creator. This is why ants and other mammals can sense their foods, danger, and environmental changes. If these lesser beings could sense provisions, contracts for safety, and live normal lives without formal education, then humans with better knowledge should have greater survival strategies. The trends and reports from various institutions of learning, high unemployment, and starvation in many countries are proof that many are out of touch in receiving the knowledge needed to progress. Inferably, there is a massive lack of divine knowledge all around us for not showing greatness in majority.

The fear of the Lord is the beginning of knowledge (Prov. 1:7; 9:10). Seemingly, other living and nonliving things must have this fear to receive the knowledge to run their causes. The sun, moon, stars, mountain, ocean, and wind do not receive instructions from people to perform dutifully;

these created things know their assignments to perform them. Every assignment has a job description, and accountability, outcome measures, coordination, and specificity are all useful components of any function. Do you know your assignments? Everyone has to be assigned something for functionality, coordination, and productivity by the Creator. All institutions have standards, measures, audit trails, manuals, and enforcement systems for compliance. You are an entity with identity and commanding power of an icon to see the future through God's eyes. The information about your mission, the power of spoken words, warnings of intruders, and the importance of forgiving others are powerful determinants of how one's life could end up.

A person refusing to acknowledge that he or she needs God's words to survive will have trouble identifying his or her reasons for existence. Such a person may also have problems obeying authority and knowing when to refuse limitations others place on him. Supervisors and leaders are there to monitor, brief, and interpret guidelines. However, there are many hidden pushbacks in life to need God's help to navigate even with the best human practice. Without wisdom and this divine knowledge, a person is more likely to let the environment, negative mindset, associates, parental influences, and other external factors dictate his or her future. For example, the advice of a well-meaning friend in good faith may not be in the best interest of the person. There are no limitations when it comes to pursuing our God-given purpose; this revelation can only be obtained from God's words.

Using David as a typical example, the opinion of his father and brothers did not count toward him becoming the king (1 Sam. 17:26–31). He was written off as a potential candidate for kingship by his own father. He was uneducated and unpolished but was spiritually savvy, was full of determination, and had the willingness to take chances, among other noble qualities. He discovered the importance of God's words to seek and reach out, seeing the future from God's angle (1 Sam. 20:12–17). Even after experiencing a breakthrough, he associated himself with positive minds like Jonathan, the son of his arch enemy. It takes an open mind to recognize that one can find innovators, inventors, and good leaders in hostile environment. David obtained great victories, support, and success by forgiving others who have offended him. Further, on several occasions he chose praise and worship rather than deploying his armies to fight the enemy. There were so many evidence-based applications of God's words in David's life for being accountable, loyal, committed, and trusting in God.

He wrote all the psalms as a testament of the lows and highs that each one of us must go through. Life ordeals are too difficult to proceed without God's help and His words, unless you want to be enlisted in the hall of failure in contrast to the hall of the famous that His association brings.

Your desire to learn will unfold the embedded logic to roleplay those functionalities across the continuum to better your surrounding.

Using the Outcome of Your Success to make Others Successful

As our world shows various signs and symptoms for reform, it becomes obvious that everyone needs a change of habit or lifestyle to develop an analytical and sacrificial mindset for viability. Life is a phase designed to require everyone to engage in continuous improvement and production, learning to do more with less in scarcity, pressing forward in adversity, and changing thought processes to become value focused for success. Too much of everything has a way of making people nonchalant; so is staying in familiar territory and doing the same routine, which is known to cause a decrease of enthusiasm. I am not sure that anyone or any enterprise, poor or rich, big or small, could succeed without any effort to increase value. Everyone has an inert drive for success; however, your success begins with an inner drive to succeed, using even economic downturn, adverse situations, cultural restrictions, risks, and negative behaviors of others to become better. How do you acquire a successful mindset? Who's responsible for making you successful? Your uncertainty in answering these questions is a nudge that you need a renewed mindset to work on your success.

People may look upon their parents, spouses, children, bosses, associates, and society to hand them success. You may wait forever on any of these categories to make you successful, to no avail (Gal. 6:4–5). True success comes from becoming who God created you to be and having what you are meant to have; thus, success is not around you but within you. Money, possessions, and fame cannot be equivocally used to measure success because of their inability to make you happy. God's seed of success is embedded inside of you, and your ability to retrieve this seed for use to accomplish assigned tasks brings success. In essence, you are responsible for growing the success seed. Your seed produces an output for others to patronize you. The value you place on yourself and the output by training, and the desensitization you acquire in the process, humbles you to relate to others (Ob. 1:3–4). Your sense of worth and value are crucial as to how you see yourself and the people God puts in your path. The sense of self comes with the boldness for knowing who you are and where you are going. The misery, pain, problems, and issues most people go through to become successful are meant to be used to minister to others for a better relationship. God affirmed this through the coming of Christ on earth to our level.

If you are wondering whether you have the language of success, read further for the two important impact duos to jumpstart your walk. Your source of impact is very important. The summation of the story is that you are created to accomplish specific tasks; hence your relationship with the task giver guarantees your success for knowing what to do (1 Thess. 3:12). Everyone starts this journey, but not everyone ends successfully, by either giving up or refusing to change attitudes to become successful (Gal. 6:7–9). True, meaningful success comes from doing what God calls you to do and having what you are meant to have for happiness, peace, wealth, and fulfillment (1 Tim. 6:6–9). A person governed by this principle seeks God to uncover his or her assignments. Venturing out on your own without putting first the well-being of others and God's will may cost you time, energy, money, and some breakdowns for operating outside the mission statement. You have the mind of Christ, the Creator of all things, to make you creative—a problem solver with faith to speak to the negative conditions because of your expectations (Heb. 2:6–8). The Holy Spirit provides guidance to move or refrain in every decision. The same Holy Spirit reveals things life throws at you for improvement, and it provides a renewed, open mind. Such a mind understands that you have to change around others and not wait for others to change.

Waiting for people to change or hand you success brings frustration and can result in you sitting in the limbo with unnecessary agony and pain (Rom. 8:20–22). Success thinkers accept changes, rejections, and criticism because God's words affirm their usefulness to be encouraged. Success thinkers are humble, patient, and compassionate for understanding the importance of these attributes to win their audience. Successful people use God's gifts to impact others to receive good measure with input. Your success is dependent on how you use what you already have to impact others (Rom. 12:6–8). Understanding your purpose helps you to labor in love and to impact others even when the flesh resists. In all, learning to relate to God by studying His words enables you to relate to others— the basic course for success. It comes with a renewed mindset to build your dreams around others; it is a life that will never be put on hold for refusing to invite laziness, temptations, and loneliness. Successful people will never quit producing and solving the problems of others, because they understand that when they do, failure is imminent.

Real success comes by pointing struggling others in your pathway to the right path in this rocky life.

Your Environment is a Threshold for Scoring Your Contributions.

The scoring board for measuring the meaningful contributions of any entity, person, or affiliation is reflective of noticeable differences to the surroundings. No matter how much investment one makes to upload one's image, one's surrounding is a relative voice that cannot be silenced. Thus, one of the goals of any person or entity is to take time to appreciate the value of people and one's surroundings. The difference that this noble action brings goes to the scoring board to create room for prosperity. People are assets and instruments for use in bringing development to society. However, when these instruments are not cleaned, upgraded, labeled, and apply properly, development is thwarted. Thus goals and scoring the differences made to your surroundings should go hand in hand. When have you last scored yourself or an entity or affiliation for making positive changes in a person, place, or an organization via bright ideas, talents, and gifts? There are goals and levels of accomplishment, but what counts the most because of its derivative blessing is how you influence others with whatever you have (1 Pet. 4:9–10). Everyone has a measure of grace relative to the talents and personal attributes that affect people, and there are places to engage in worthy causes each day (Matt. 25:22–23). Have you considered why you walk, talk, laugh, and smile the way you do? Whatever skills and attributes you possess are meant to inspire others to aim higher. You wouldn't know how you are doing in your parameter without scoring yourself. There are many wonders in you to influence others and to never have a dull moment in life. Scoring is very decisive to award contract, diploma, and certification, and to determine who wins in the Olympics, Super Bowl, and other tournaments. Scoring is a powerful measure for sizing up your receipt for giving out your time, talents, and personal attributes, for reasonable services (1 Thess. 5:14). Scoring is very important when you wish to make something out of this life.

The fact of the matter is that people usually panic when the word "scoring" is mentioned. Perhaps people do not want to know what they are putting out in their zeal to work for themselves, as a display of personal affluence. If this characteristic describes you, consider yourself an audience in a retreat camp of the imperfect, having a curiosity to explore the newfound principle to excel. In retrospect, the self-scoring template is very simple. However, we complicate life by piling up too many things on our plate to miss the core ingredients that drive total prosperity. The core ingredients are your positive influences, which are what you have given out in life to inspire others to hope. The questions to you are: Do your daily dealings with people, in words or actions, accomplish this purpose? Do people feel defeated, elevated, or motivated after being with you? Are your actions or words giving others personal enrichment? Your scoring on this core measure is instrumental to whatever you are getting. It is a positive energy that rejuvenates your mind; life has meaning for adding meaning to the lives of others. You are given a new mercy and goodness every morning to score higher on this measure daily. Life is about giving your noble services, being mindful that your actions receive reactions and rewards from God and people (Luke 6:38). It is a principle that cannot be broken. The principle of value is the core in choosing what to do, where to go, and with whom to associate. The choice should not be made to devalue people and things He created, but with a scope and timing that only God's revelation brings. You may believe that you do not devalue anyone. We all devalue things and people by looking down via our actions and words (2 Tim. 2:1618; 1 Tim. 6:20–21).

You may be looking down on your neighborhood by silent behavior or by not participating in activities to impact the residents positively. Your earnest self- scoring calculates what you are depriving others and of what you are being deprived (Luke 6:38–43). God will multiply what you have released willingly for others to benefit from, to give them back to you in multiple measures. Thus the way you show mercy, kindness, forgiveness, empathy, and encouragement to others is very vital to your receiving same from God (Gal. 6:2). You may be piling up pardon, encouragement, and bright ideas on your desk. Yesterday's goodness and mercy become stale the next day. You may be piling up things that could have helped someone to advance in life, which also creates a barricade for yourself (Heb. 3:13, 13:3). Your association with people should always inspire them to hope. Can you be counted upon to make contributions via noble suggestions in school PTA, your place of employment, and meetings for worthy causes? Are you shying away from anything that requires your time, support, and contributions to better your world? Have you forgotten that there are miraculous healing and innovative technology taking place daily? You can extend your hands to fallen heroes and get them to hope again by talking them into to seeking professional help. These are just a few examples of positive actions that qualify you as your neighbor's keeper.

Every hero in the past may have done things of which he or she was not proud. It took God's grace not be apprehended. Helping others to avoid the pitfalls as an individual who was down on that memory lane is an act of giving back for total prosperity. God sees His attributes in people that do things to better others (Deut. 26:9–11). Your willingness to share your time, good ideas, and talents to impact lives are various ways of giving to activate the exchange principle of receiving—a powerful force for obtaining wealth, health, peace, joy, and fulfillment. Any mindset, habit, or behavior that prevent you from deriving this exchange affects your growth (Rom. 14:13). Just be mindful that when you release what you have in your hand daily, God releases what He has daily for you (Luke 6:38; Rev. 3:20). The acceptance of His personal invitation to digest his daily words for your food for thought will provide vision and enable you to become fruitful, healthy, and purposeful, receiving strength for waiting and being waited on by His angels assigned to you. The analysis here is that dining with the almighty God provides you with the living bread and water, and the best fruits from the tree of life. The conversation at the dinner table gives you bright ideas to go to the untapped areas as a first responder for breakthrough. To top it all, your imagination will run wild when you understand that the cook of this daily dinner is God Himself, and your waiters are his assigned angels(Ps. 23:5–6; Heb. 1:10–14). Even a bear will hug and never let go of anyone who provides it with goodies and mercy in the morning and a conference call dinner at night. The revelations of the above will ignite you to wise up and to see greatness in everyone and everything you have made small. This authority and declaration of freedom is your noble action that will bring improvement, wealth, unity, peace, and health to your world, in the glory of God (John 15:15–17).

Your impact tells the world what you are made of.

Excitement, Joy, Flexibility and Connectivity are derived as You Impact Others

The challenging outlook of life could dampen the outlook of a person who refuses to help others by choice. The lack of understanding that making an impact is one's way to recovery, restoration, wealth, health, happiness, and fulfillment has kept so many in the limbo and deprived. Making an impact is the most available, accessible, and simple tool to enjoy life on earth while maximizing output. This tool can be used anywhere, anytime, and by anybody to achieve great results. A person who truly understands the power of positive impact is unmoved by the changing behavior of others and challenges, but uses them as opportunities to challenge others to be optimistic. It is imperative that the individual recognizes that seeking ways and means to work on character, relationships, and skills to better others promotes finance, motivation, and health for body, mind, and soul. However, the opposite is the case when many seek for employers, spouses and friends to provide everything, with a resultant lack of fulfillment, joy, and impact. A huge pile of joy liberates one to glow and blossom even with physical disability, limitations, bondage, or lack. Becoming mindful of others wherever you are, with a willingness to assist, brings joy. The derived joy is your harmless stimulant to strengthen, elevate, and build up people and things with a return on investment. Your impact leaves an imprint that may linger for generations to benefit your loved ones.

There have been many unrealistic claims that power, money, and controlling others provides joy. Taking advice on how to manage your life speaks volumes—the richest and wisest man can become controlled by things and people later in life. Anyone can be overpowered by the fleshy body to the detriment of the power house, the mind. The eyes and ears, for example, are fleshy parts of the body that need to be tamed, or they will affect your destiny. When a wealthy, skilled professional fails to discipline the impulsive eyes and makes a terrible decision, then the mind has been defeated. The ear is meant to receive all information, however not all information is good for you. In essence, if left uncontrolled, the fleshy body will always want satisfaction contrary to the mind and the spirit within. Joy is always affected when the spirit growth is ignored. No wonder the mind could buy suggested ideas in a person controlled by a fleshy body. You are provided with a survival kit for security and to make an impact; inside this survival kit are modifiers, maps, mission statements, and a procedure manual for guidance. The manual is God's words, the Bible. The modifiers are things unique to you, revealed by the spirit as you involve Christ to fit in, make amends, blend in, endure, and go through the ups and downs in every situation. Your failure to apply appropriate modifiers will produce a general result for using general expectations to configure your life. You can never make an impact listening to generalists or hanging around most crowds who are clueless of your makeup and assignment on earth. Your mind has to be renewed to think impact, love, patience, and commitment to others.

We are all beneficiaries of modern researchers that have created preventive and curative medicine from the noble impacts of others. There are more noble prizes and millions of lives to be saved, and major improvements to be made, if only each and every one of us will tune in to hear the cries of others. These outcries sound louder at home, work, prisons, hospitals, schools, and more during hard times. Everyone needs a daily touch to discover, recover, recoup, network, and make a U-turn for good. We are all students of the impact academy, no matter our level of education, gender, race, and nationality; we should help one another fight the battle of the mind. An idle or neglected mind becomes a medium to grow bacteria that could invade its surroundings. Everyone wants to succeed. However, refraining from doing what the body wants is tough and counterproductive. This is where the experiences and discipline of those with spiritual maturity become vital to go after others for rebounds. The fleshy body on its own can never commit to anything or stay in a relationship. It is very authoritative, careless, and greedy, and it does not know how to avoid pitfalls until it has fallen into the ditch. Even when in the ditch, it may still crave addictive, self-injurious, and distant behaviors in which to hide.

In short, the body fights every good thing coming your way for being noncommittal, selfish, territorial, and self-seeking. You are created as a facilitator, caretaker, and builder, rich and famous as you adopt an impact lifestyle. This lifestyle produces a smile in you and others. Your smile will convert the frowns, depressive, destructive, and hopeless thoughts of others into meaning, not only enriching you but developing your surroundings this year.

Your environment is a real feedback on how well you are doing.

Maximizing Your Return on Investment by Investing in People

There are multiple reasons why people created to take charge experience abundance as well as failure for being controlled by things they are meant to control. Everyone on the planet has the propensity to multiply, replenish, and have dominion over the fish of the sea, fowl of the air, and every living and moving thing on earth. Every herb, tree, fruit, seed, and animal is given to you to care for, feed on, and develop. Your understanding that you are created to multiply, increase, grow, advance, progress, and take dominion, giving names to things and people, is a powerful force to propel you to get up every day and to make the required impact. Increment, enlargement, progress, and advancement are included in your package upon arrival on earth to be saddened, demoralized, and burdened with hollow ideas for lacking creativity (Gen. 1:28–30). Things may not be happening in your life and neighborhood because of your failure to foresee progress and development in the technical schools, healthcare centers, healthy crops, herbs, livestock, and jobs all around you (1 Tim. 6:9–10). You are responsible for discovering the potential of people around you to build up.

The Lord God will not advance supplies and tools for development and growth unless there is a capable person to receive and care for it (Gen. 1:5). Your roadmap for success begins with recognition of the authority to take dominion and identify your area of domain with vested interest. Building a better future entails finding ways and means to care for others and things. The root cause of most sufferings, challenges, and deprivations may be as a result of parents, individuals, and leaders not caring for things and people God has entrusted in their care. God will provide funding through people with earnest efforts. The fact of the matter is that you must act like a person interested in his or her area of dominion to care and nurture. A person of vested interest in this dominion cannot let things like herbs, food, and gadgets to dominate him or her to cause him or her to lose control. It is a special privilege to care for life and things. You are given a delegated authority to make declarations, standing in the gap for people as God's ambassador; it requires love, humility, kindness, fairness, and a genuine caring of people. The clear understanding of this role reshapes your thoughts to act as an agent of change, hope, and increase for others (Phil. 2:3–4). We sometimes frustrate God by staying in comfort zones, ignoring our responsibilities. No wonder we are forcefully moved here and there for better opportunities by the Creator (Deut. 1:6–7). The Creator recognizes the negative effects of sedentary life and use all kinds of mover-and-shaker techniques to get some caretakers to respond.

Everyone wants a good life, but not everyone is willing to care for the earth to earn the good life. Acquiring relevant skills and being compliant, committed, and trustworthy are important attributes of a good caretaker. These characteristics are earnest signs that you are ready to accept the assignment and can make important decisions that impact lives. Order, security, safety, and excellent track records are pluses for any caretaker. An abusive, depleted, destructive, arrogant, lazy, wicked, oppressive personality disqualifies a good caretaker. People are God's interest and should be mindful and guarded by Him. Children are God's special ways of introducing needed skills to replace an aging workforce. Thus, taking time to invest in children to better serve the society is one of the ways to pursue God's interest. It is a rewarding sacrifice to bring up your children to take responsibility, respect authority, and be community-development oriented. Parents, schoolteachers, spiritual leaders, and mentors play great roles in shaping the mindsets and career goals of the next generation.

Being patient with people who do not act or look like you, showing kindness to others needing your services at your job, and words of encouragement are sources of positive impact to people going through emotional, social, and financial struggles. Healthy exchanges of encouraging words will definitely improve efficiency at all levels. For example, a great surgeon who stood up for eight hours doing a surgery will be energized and inspired to operate again the next day if he or she receives a few kind words that he or she was appreciated. We are known to give our best when we are appreciated and are told that how good we are in deeds. Great leaders, producers, inventors, and technicians have been known to emerge from people with past challenges, upon receiving the necessary help. Investing in people to turn around has a thousand times return on investment (Deut. 1:11; Luke 6:38). Joining others to establish schools, walking for the homeless and other foundations to raise funds, and providing internships and summer jobs for youths are a few examples of how you can invest in the future. Your successful breakthrough is assured and simplified when you align your interests to that of the Creator—the people (Gal. 6:2–9). Making an impact is a rewarding and profitable lifestyle; it is a universal and user-friendly tool available for everyone to be used anywhere and anytime to build relationships, families, children, life, society, and any nation. I strongly believe that the majority of us are performing beneath our maximum potential. Everyone has love, kindness, encouraging words, and thank-yous, to say the least. You can use these to prop up that chief executive officer at the bank, the teacher waiting at the bus stop, and more. We are all human regardless of our position, title, status, and upbringing, with feelings, emotions, and supportive needs that could leave anyone of us miserable to underperform with burdens and crises. This is the good news that the love of God is all about: seeing others as friends and a social network for coordination in building a healthy and wealthy society.

People are your active doors to stay active to fulfill your purpose for victory.

How to Become a Reformer to Manage Time and Resources

It is important to calculate the meaningful use of your time and resources for waste management, productivity, and possible decline. Whereas there may be an overall decline in employment rate globally, recovery follows a decline as people look for alternatives. Without good measures and honest people keeping you in check, you may walk this life wasting away. Opportunists thrive on others and society during good and bad economies, lacking knowledge of the benefits of meaningful use (Hab. 2:6–7). Meaningful use of your time and resources is a productive lifestyle for success and fulfillment; it adds value to your life to do same to your environment. Use timing to study your world and to effectively plan (Luke 12:54–59), because it protects you from low self-esteem, isolation, ignorance, and deprivation for applying your time and resources to make valuable contributions. It leaves you with little or no room for worries, idleness, gossip, and slander. Meaningful use of your time and resources is a sign of growth, maturity, wisdom, discipline, and sound management approved by God for mankind (Jer. 17:10–11). Have you realized that when you are broke, jobless, and in a money crunch, that is the time you dig deeper into your freezer or closet to find a forgotten goody? What's more, you give your brain challenging thoughts when you are hard pressed to bring out the jewel you are made of, as the dry hot weather cracks the nutshells to bring out edible nuts.

Even though we are experiencing a budget cut, program down-sizing, and high unemployment, most employers are in dire need of policy, infrastructure, and productivity reformers. Time and resource management is very important in our turbulent world; it calls for measures to address waste management in every area of your life. You can lose focus in life when everything you want is at your doorstep. You will not know how to handle crises, scarcity, pressure, and surprises when you stay in your familiars (Prov. 21:5, 17). Your ability to manage time and resources makes you a converter, navigator, and adaptor to bring treasure from trash, filling up the valleys with plain ground to cultivate. It is obvious that the more time you have to play, gossip, and roam the street aimlessly, the less time you have to reason in your thoughts. Cost, quality, connectivity, scrutiny, and security are all paramount to stepping up to meet the challenges of the twentieth century. There is always a reason behind God's actions. He purposely allowed the earth to be dark and hopeless with no form to reform it (Gen. 1:1–3). Similarly, anything that is void in your life can be reformed. The pit and prison did not paralyze Joseph; he emerged a winner because he knew his God (Gen. 37:24).

Society and people will put you down sometimes. Calculated insults await the rich, poor, bad, and good alike. Rejection, snubbing, and ostracizing are included in your orientation package at every level. Unless you learn to navigate, joggle, blend, and ignore negative people and certain comments, you may walk this life feeling persecuted, rejected, and alienated. Nothing can insulate you from facing challenges, pain, disappointment, pressure, and accusation—except your preparedness spiritually to handle them (Prov. 17:18). Poverty and riches are not your enemies but are opportunities to apply your time and resources to live a purposeful life. Poverty has a way of making people think that the rich are their enemies. It is not about how much time and resources you have that brings meaning to life, but how you utilize them to accomplish God's purpose.

Joseph was born to save the entire world from famine (Gen. 41:56–57). He decided to focus on his purpose to ignore the enslavement, accusations, and betrayals. Emotional torment about wasting in your relationship with God has haunted so many, causing them to use things and the pursuit of a lesser god to fill in the gap. Your closeness to God teaches you to love without judging, ridiculing, and persecuting. The above steps enable you to meaningfully manage the time and His resources at your disposal. Without God, a successful person may become too pompous and full of himself or herself and will climb the rooftop for notoriety, losing everything due to a lack of discipline. Without God, a person experiencing problems may see no way out and be so desperate to try destructive things and or lose hope.

It takes the knowledge of God in your life to make better use of your time on earth (Prov. 2:6–12). The knowledge of His words puts meaning to life as you become the salt and light of the earth. It humbles you to forgive and utilize your time as God's caretaker on earth; it enables you to hear your conscience and to avoid waste, lingering, distraction, and diversion for a joyful end.

Challenges provide opportunities for careful observations, analysis and deductions to maximize outcome.

Understanding Your Position of Prominence for Preparations to avoid Impulsive Decisions

The utter belief that you have of being defenseless to issues, preventing you to take dominion, is due to your unbelief that God has restored your prominence. It costs God nothing to create you and the world He loves (Gen. 1:3–4, 26–27), but it costs God the death of His beloved son to not only save your soul but to save you from those things that are preventing you to reach the height He has placed you (Heb. 9:12; Matt. 1:21, 17:5). Traditionally, predators, deceivers, and gold-diggers go to prominent and profitable places to look for treasures. Inconsiderate people and other spiritual forces engage your mind as their battleground to deceive you into making bad decisions. This is why it is difficult to understand the mindset of a mother that drove herself and her five children into a river. The same ambiguity exists as you try to understand the mindset of a father who shot himself and the entire family after he lost a job. There is also difficulty in understanding the mindset of a person using alcohol, dangerous drugs, and others substances to attain a euphoric high. Added to this decision-making puzzle are individuals walking away from their homes for erroneous feelings of losing their places. Most of us have mistakenly walked out of our jobs, relationship, assignments, and more for various reasons of feeling out of place. Some youths have also walked away from homes for various reasons, such as losing their freedom after being reprimanded by good parents. It is the desire of good parents that their children aspire to greater heights, and parents will incessantly warn them of appealing but destructive things of life.

The feeling of losing your position in life is real; it cuts across race, gender, age. and socioeconomic status. Every human being is created to make choices based on conviction at every given point in time. The decision you make is based on whether or not the information you received is right or wrong. A chain smoker with COPD is actually convinced that cigarette smoking does no harm. A manipulator that feels elevated for manipulating others. The need to achieve prominence is inert because we are created to take dominion. This desire also comes with the fear of losing out, being wrongly engage in contrary activities, and losing dominion at last (Gen. 3:6–12, 23–24) Attaining a position of prominence is a gift from God; none of us did anything to deserve it. Your opinion was not solicited as to your skin color, gender, talent, and biological parents (Rom. 9:19–21). You are placed by God's choice, as He placed Adam and Eve in the Garden before the fall (Gen. 2:15–17). Similarly, ignoring the warnings of the Creator against modern predators, identity thieves, and hijackers will displace you from high places meant for you. The predators are masters in their fields to approach you openly. Mind games have always been used as effective routes to engage culprits to make destructive decisions themselves. No un-renewed mind is ever equipped to handle the twisting, tantalizing, hidden, and euphoric tactics of these life predators (2 Cor. 10:4–5). However, renewing your mind comes from hearing God's words and applying them to your life.

Jesus Christ left the throne to counteract everything you could possibly face in life (Isa. 9:6). This is a Good Friday gift to those whose belief followed by Easter Sunday, a celebration of restoration to prominence. Easter also marks the return of Christ to the throne, making intercession for you (Rom. 8:26–34). You are now covered by Christ's righteousness as you make honest efforts to learn a new walk as a born-again. The transfer of His righteousness makes you an heir to attract envy and jealousy of the adversary. The Holy Spirit is given to every heir for protection against every mind twister. Studying the Bible is important to mastering God's words to counter thoughts of failure, fear, hate, hopelessness, and powerlessness to victory, faith, love, hope, and power to stay prominent. Your new place of prominence is a shift of position to disallow familiar others and things to control you. Your new status will gradually lessen your dependence on those things on which you have previously depended to make it (1 John 5:4). You will no longer listen to destructive suggestions because you'll have the Holy Spirit. Hopelessness is an enemy of us all for not engaging the Holy Spirit.

Restoration to prominence calls for a walk of forgiveness, kindness, love, patience, and purpose. It took more than a walk for Christ to restore you to prominence, however total recovery is dependent upon you walking boldly without intimidation to get back whatever you have lost by faith. There is no dull moment for a person with the revelation of God's will on earth (John 6:63). The revealed words will change rebellious youths into productive, next-generation adults. It will transform you into a peace maker, mentor, and watch person for your family and the individuals God placed in your life to impact (Prov. 8:21; Deut. 6:6–7). Riches, titles, and other traditional positions can never be equated to your position in the one-to-one relationship with the king of kings.

Your position as a leader attracts others to imitate your walk, work and actions to follow suit.

Lessons on Persistence to Obtain and Transfer Inheritance to Generations

The season of Easter is the story of a persistence of a loving father doing whatever it takes to not only reestablish the lost relationship but to also restore inheritance to generations. It is the story of an advocate sticking to difficult, painful, shameful, humiliating, and yet a pious job description to discharge and acquit those who believe of all charges, needed to obtain their inheritance. The lesson to be learned from this act of obedience and submission is that it takes persistence to handle every task in every field, because of your love for others and of God's care for people He has put in your path. Persistence is also inert, in that little children perfect so well in this, wearing down parents and those around to get their needs. Your enemy will also give in when you persist, mounting pressure in your pursuit to get what you are looking for, not because he or she wants to, but to have the peace that comes from honoring your request. The Creator has also established in His words that your persistence in asking Him will definitely get His attention to grant your request, unlike those who do not ask or who give up easily. The few pointers outlined above are your tips to use this principle to run your life, starting with your home, ensuring that your children become men and women to drive the future, outshining and stepping up to help you become a voice when yours is losing its tone. Persistence is also important in obtaining provision and restoration from God, which is needed to live a fruitful life.

Persistence has a deeper meaning for coming from the very deep to drive the meaning of one's existence. Persistence enables you to see a bigger picture, the light in the tunnel, the gain in pain, and the triumph in trial to pursue regardless of the status quo. God has set a perfect example, persisting to make you victorious in victimization, an overcomer in an overcoming situation, and seeing you as an arrow in His hand to travel far and wide, making a noble impact. You are an arrow in God's eye, for use to alleviate the pain of others, developing your skill sets to meet the needs of others via persistence. Easter has painted a picture for all entities to step down to hear, feel, mingle, and identify with the people in their care for grass-roots problem solving. The season also exposes emotional scars, torments, inflicted wounds of others, false accusations, betrayals, and sorrow as ordeals, and anyone making a positive impact will face the very people to persevere to the glorious end. It is not a pleasant surprise that as needy people, our needs, unknown to most of us, can become very antagonistic to those divinely chosen to help us. Negative experiences and deprivation may have tendencies to bring out some behaviors from personal encounters, belief systems, and limited knowledge, for anyone encountering others to study the background of clienteles for better outcome. Easter marked the grand finale to use the information for better relationship and advocacy for you and me.

Another elemental factor about persistence is that it is relationship driven. God knows the importance of stepping up and developing persistence through relationships that begin at home. A home is God's first institution to develop relationships through perseverance and patience, ignoring the ugly, weak, and dragging sides of family members in dealing with each other. A home is the beginning of the formation of a relationship whereby two total strangers come together to drive vision and help members to reach out for fulfillment. A home is also the first school to learn to relate to others and to receive and give out love, strength, encouragement, help, and advice. People also learn to take risks, develop trust, focus on the finish line, maintain the family's image, and persist in restoring all relationships, even with tolerable bruises and betrayals of members. This is the main reason Jesus Christ came to restore fragmented relationships between you and God. It is very obvious that you are created to relate to God, to obtain your mission statement, and to derive your personal inheritance. Adam and Eve severed the perfect relationship, and that has affected us all to lack and live in our present sufferings.

Finally, there is something phenomenal about this relationship that money, fame, title, and position have not been able to fill. It is an inert vacuum that has driven many people to seek ways and means to fill, to no avail; they are without the love of God that teaches them to show true love, which is needed to be happy. The disconnection and missing link for the absence of this relationship may result in not seeing the meaning to life, lacking the meaningful use of our talents to impact others—the very essence of everyone's existence.

The pursuit of fame and position at the very extreme and void of relationship may alienate the noble supportive others .

Preparing for Tomorrow Today with What You Don't Know You Have

You are empowered, as a living soul, to handle life and replenish things that have run out, using personal attributes and talents to make deposits for future withdrawals. Mistakes, past failures, misfortunes, natural disasters, and wrong choices will never keep the world stagnant (Gen. 8:22). You are empowered as God's image to use even the bad decisions of yesterday to make good ones tomorrow. Poor judgments and bad seeds and investments of the past can convert into good. The irrevocable words of the Creator have established such to ignore the chaos to keep producing (Isa. 55:11; Gen. 1:27–29). You are thus empowered to envision future growth, eliminate waste, and adapt to the evolving needs of your world. You are the one to recognize needs and to come up with suitable communication, training, and delivery. You are the one to take God's words at heart and to refrain from panic when an old era is being shaken for a new one to emerge (Deut. 32:46–47). Obedience to God's words will keep you from all extremes, thus preventing you from falling from the cliff or taking a nose dive into the pit (Eccles. 7:16–18). Scientifically, socially, and physiologically, anything at the very extreme—such as, temperament, vital signs, habits, and more—becomes a problem. God's words keep you in check for your good. His words provide blessings, healing, protection, and provision, and serve as a power conduit to recharge your battery when you are running low. Every provision has been made by God to empower you to multiply, produce, and replenish at all seasons (Gen. 9:6–7). Your disobedience and unbelief may rob your recovery.

Everything stationary and moving on the earth and in the sea has been given to you. Becoming creative to launch technology with appropriate monitoring is in your job description as an image bearer; this includes involving the next generation for continuity, adapting to changes, and sharing information and hardware. The empowerment of God's words provides discernment, wisdom, character reformation, and discipline for effective work flow toward recovery, maximum production, and delivery. The pressures and frustrations of people around you can squeeze out some negatives to corrupt your words. Words have the power to perpetuate recession, poverty, and hardship in the environment. You must prime yourself to see the big picture of unfolding events that will make your world better (Rom. 12:2).

It may be impossible to withstand the temptations and pressures of your surroundings, especially people without spiritual maturity (Luke 22:34). You have to read the ordeals of Job to understand the surmounting pressure of losing everything without giving in and giving up (Job 1). It is only by God's words that you can have hope, because His promises of the future enable you to endure hardship and betrayals (Num. 23:19–20). Experts in every field go through a series of tests after training to become licensed, certified, and accredited. Such empowerment comes with dismantling and dealing with unfamiliar territories. Preparing for empowerment tests begins with staying calm, being watchful, and not mistakenly accusing others, thereby devaluing the very entities you are meant to uphold. No person or group of people historically has moved to the next level without facing their giants. There is always a giant before every breakthrough to rejoice during those dark moments. Cheap talk is for the weak; the wise always reach deep within to retrieve real substance, ignoring cheap talk and blame games. Job reached within to pray for his friends, forgiving his wife because of his belief in God's promises for recovery (Job 42:1–13). Your belief should be checked when you fail to recover from what is God's will for you. Are you a contributor of your stagnancy by inactivity and not forgiving yourself and others?

We will reap the seeds of today, tomorrow (Gal. 6:7). Each of us has seeds in the form of talents, attributes, or gifts to sow in others. For example, patience, mercy, encouragement, kindness, and time are seeds that could be sown now for harvest later (2 Cor. 9:6). The impact of your actions is felt when you fail to streamline spending and refuse to engage your thought to become creative, to do more with less resources as you replenish depleted things. The impact is also felt when you fail to help children be their best. The lean approach to life involves paying bills on time and adhering to rules to avoid costly penalties. The impact of your empowerment will be felt when you use every opportunity as teachable moments to encourage, advise, teach, and correct others. It will be a win-win when you become empowered to provide tools, information, and a proper environment for others to make informed choices, contracting for safety both spiritually and physically.

You have the ability to use adversity to season yourself to withstand various kinds of professional, social and environmental seasonal changes.

The Importance of Restoring Inevitable Net-Work for Survival

The demand on life can be very overwhelming when you fail to network with people at the endpoint of your beginning point. The endpoint people are those who have already attained the level of knowledge and skills for which you are vying (Josh. 1:1–7). The "to do" list of this life is very lengthy for one to not tap the wisdom of mentors, teachers, and skillful others, even when they are annoying. Life is not meant to be spent navigating alone without being touched or touching others. Readiness, cost, and process impact are involved in becoming a victorious person. There is an incredible growth with limitless opportunities when you are flexible with a broad view that others are co-contributors, partners, clienteles, information feeders, and mentors in your life. No one could have an ideal environment with attributes, skills, finance, and support to meet all needs. Mentors, teachers, and authoritative figures have been aligned by God for you, if only you will recognize and listen to their counsel (Ruth 3). Many influential people making great impact in the society understood that they couldn't have made it without others (Esther 2:10). Cell phones and other modern gadgets can never become a direct replacement of mentorship, teaching, coaching, and hope that significant others bring to our world. The advent of technology may have provided distant social network and information access, but it should not deprive people, especially children, of the vital personal touch. The principle and process of structured environment such as schools, with caring about others, provides such a need.

Many people celebrating great success today could attest of the impact of mentors and teachers in their pursuit. It is important to realize that as we celebrate the pros of technology, we should also brace ourselves to not feel too comfortable, hugging the Internet and cell phones, thereby replacing them with mentors, teachers, coaches, and skill mavericks around us (Heb. 13:17). Individuals who for obvious reasons shy away from people of impact may experience stagnation if they are out of touch. The fact of the matter is that you will have many challenges when you try to handle everything on your shopping list by yourself. You will be ineffective as a stand-alone when you try to grow your own crop or milk your own cow, refusing to relate and to be impacted by others (Luke 12:35–38). Securing privacy and highly prized possessions may be important, but ignoring the fact that you're limiting yourself to Blackberry and iPhones, Internet, and video-monitored mansions will not go away soon. However, it can never be a win-win for anyone to neglect the Creator's guide for real success and for staying successful. You can never fail when you operate in love during your link with others (1 Cor. 13:4–8). You need people, and they also need you to make contributions by connecting your dots on planet earth. You need the services of others to enable you to focus solely on what you are good at. Doing what you do best and networking with others will eliminate time spent doing things outside your best effort. The process, cost, and time to train in every area—to be your own physician, manger, producer, lawyer, architect, and share cropper—may take your lifetime to materialize. Thus, your strength and gifts are desperately needed, as you desperately need others. The prize for not networking with others is as huge as a stand-alone whose skills and touch fail to rub others (2 Pet. 1:5–8).

From the practical viewpoint, the readiness for anyone to become a successful, self-sufficient person without anyone else is impossible. Hence, any mental picture or suggestion to alienate the self for any reason at all will never be the best practice to live a victorious life. Such a lifestyle is just another broken link to deprive the self of others' impact, and vice versa (Prov. 18:9). It is beneficial to refrain from fighting the wrong fight of defeat via isolation, because of negative experiences and past failures. The fight of faith to restore lost dignity, wealth, health, and influence is available to those who belief that "they are now more than conquerors" (Rom. 8:37). The impact of God's love is so exponential that it turns you around in every aspect to link up good and impact others for a joyful, successful, fulfilling, and healthy ending.

Your best and my best for taking time to do our best provide the best for the society.

Obeying Rules, Regulations and Using Common Sense Principles to improve Health, Wealth and Impact

L ife is too complex and full of contingencies to make the right sacrifices for victory. No matter how people and other external factors influence your life, you are still answerable for your day-to-day actions. People may intimidate or pressure you to make sacrifices for their benefits (1 Sam. 15:22–24). However any sacrifice in absence of God's words may lack His blessing. You are responsible for coming up with the best practices in making sacrifices. Businesses, nations, and individuals are responsible for measuring their progresses and performances based on their sacrifices. Security is also a part of this process. Large amounts of money are being spent on security and other intrusion protective systems because of the non-sacrificial characteristic of most people. Despite measures to establish multilayered security systems, risks still exist because of people's indifference to the harms that a breech could cause. Humans are the most important and the weakest link for an entity's success or failure. As such, God has focused on people using the Ten Commandments and the prophets to establish a culture of obedience in the past; this is because building a culture of obedience to God's words is the solution for averting attacks, risks, and challenges that life presents. People still shun God's blowing trumpet via the Holy Spirit to obey His words to be healthy, wealthy, and worry-free.

Living a disobedient life has a way of adding more threats to an already challenging environment. For example, involving oneself in criminal activities to provide for the self and family becomes a new line of threat, because you are not at peace with the self, the law, and God (Heb. 13:5–6). Many sophisticated ways are used by adversaries to gain access to homes, businesses, and your resources. It then becomes your sacrificial makeover to either obey the law of the land, which mimics God's words, to run your life or put the lives of others at risks. An Internet hacker seeking information is clueless of the wound he or she inflicts on people.

Stick to the Golden Rule, which is God's way and is fair practice, a win-win. The Golden rule simply employs you to treat others the way you want to be treated (Matt. 7:12). This rule is a higher level of sacrifice against social proliferation, cultural insensitivity, and other offensive human behavior. It is a fundamental principle sacrifice against oppression and labeling others directly or indirectly to rob them of their dignity. Love is that embodiment of a higher sacrificial lifestyle with a multilayered protection against any threat. It is the agape love with an all-inclusive, layered protection to keep your life, business, and family protected from every spiritual and physical hackers for years to come (2 Sam. 21:7) Love is the fulfillment of all laws associated with many benefits (Rom. 13:8–12) One of the benefits of sacrificial love is having various layers of security from God to catch your attackers. Love also has a way of deflating most potential attackers ahead of time. Even when you experience missed attacks for divine reasons, the agape love of God provides you with the grace needed to handle the situations.

The victory and growth of every society is dependent on the sacrifices of the people. Sacrificial lifestyle appeals to God, who is also sacrificial in nature (John 3:16). It is an obedient lifestyle to not only obey God but to obey rules and regulations at home and in your place of employment. Becoming a living sacrifice is s reflection of spiritual maturity, whereby an individual sees himself or herself as God sees him or her. It is a life of humility, accountability, and responsibility (Rom. 12:3). It is a transformed life safeguarded against failure for fellowshipping with God and yielding to the Holy Spirit (1 Cor. 9:24–27). Sacrificial lifestyle not only inspires trust but extends trust to others. People who do not like to commit to anything will have a change of heart upon dealing with a sacrificial person. There is a great tendency for people who do not want to trust you initially to change their minds when you make sacrifices without ulterior motives. Your living sacrifice is love in action that brings trust, joy, health, and wealth.

Your obedience to common rules create opportunities for employment, promotion, deployment and prosperity.

Seeing Greatness in Your Environment for Meaningful Planning

There is a tendency for people to associate success with money, power, and material wealth, and to celebrate such overlooking surroundings, as the major source of fulfillment. Wisdom and the love for people are important tools to prosper and enjoy the outcome of your labor. Success can be mistakenly measured by material and personal gains, which may not reveal the inner joy and peace. Wisdom is a gift from God used to impact people to whom your destiny is connected (Prov. 1:2–7); any disconnect from not visualizing the need to relate to these individuals may cause a missing link. The missing link could create a vacuum for people to use work, alcohol, drugs, gambling, and more to fill the void, to no avail. Furthermore, without wisdom it is very easy to become careless, greedy, arrogant, and highly opinionated, and to disconnect from the very people you are meant to impact. Achievement, pride, and overconfidence can cause a pitfall from failing to obtain feedback from the feeder sources; the feeder sources are those individuals whose profiles and vital information you need for your planning. Pride has a tendency to prevent the culprits from seeking advice and solutions to identified problems. Celebration of success and achievement, without sensitivity to the people you are destined to impact, could lead to seclusion of the self. The self is known to be a separator and selfish as it sounds. This was the experience of Solomon. The response given by the wisest, richest, and most innovative man that has ever lived, "I hated life" (Eccles. 1:17), was mind-boggling to people who admired him. This honest answer painted a picture of excluding God and people divinely connected to one's life.

Solomon's success, influence, and notoriety blossomed when he applied God's wisdom to rule the people. He enjoyed peace, wealth, health, and vision by putting God in the middle of all things (2 Chron. 9:22–28). He experienced physical and mental well-being until he shifted his focus to materials things (Prov. 16:18–20). Thus, from that point onward, everything he did—which included constructing his own beach, swimming pools, music orchestra, and mansions—were all meaningless and brought him misery (Eccles. 2:1–18). As expressed by him, the thought of leaving super-accomplishments, royalties, innovations, and wealth to family members who may not take care of them deprived him of sleep and joy. The same feeling is still plaguing many lives today. However, when Solomon recovered from his disconnect, he wisely advised everyone out there to acknowledge God as the giver of wealth. He continued to emphasize that humility would not only help individuals to focus on their visions but would enable them to use their talents, wealth, and positions to impact others (Eccles. 5, 12:13–14).

You have been given the needed talents to survive. However, developing those talents for divine purpose and obtaining wisdom is your responsibility. Operating in divine purpose is your humility at work to receive additional material things, peace, and joyful and long life. This lifestyle enables you to impact and empathize with others needing your grace, mercy, and privileges for receiving such to become successful. A successful wise person will always recall that others such as teachers, neighbors, friends, mentors, and God contributed to the success. Such recalls will humble you to appreciate those inexplicable opportunities and near-miss negative situations from which you were spared. Nonetheless, your vision is tied to godly wisdom. With it, you are well able to see your area of domain, people to network to, and hidden resources and opportunities (Gen. 13:14–17). You are able to see greatness in your surroundings and to appreciate the value (Luke 24:13–31). Wisdom also comes with patience to wait for the right time, thereby lessening your worries over things you cannot control. The mixture of patience, wisdom, and humility is an energizer to do daily chores, joyfully avoiding restlessness with great return on investment.

It is in your best interest to put God in the middle of everything you do. According to King Solomon, you may be playing a fool to refuse the wisdom of someone who has the whole world in the palm of His hand. The perspectives, resources, plans, and mission statements come from Him; He does not need any material thing from you (John 14:1–2, 21:1–11; Ps. 104:1–4). The amazing thing is that the earth is His footstool. A tornado that can level the entire city listens to Him. Thus it pays to read His word and accept His grace through Christ for continued vision, connectivity, peace, happiness, health, power, protection, and authority to care for people and things he has entrusted to you. This grace has stooped down for you, where doctrines have failed, to conquer anything that may be preventing you from seeing the greatness in you. God will not deny anything from a person who uses the outcome of this greatness to impact others with humility in godliness (Eccles. 2:26).

A mission driven life is a mission accomplished life.

What Is Your Next Level?

Your next higher level depends on many factors such as the company you keep, your expectations and resources, encouragement of others, and a constant examination of yourself to ascertain the effective usage of the present to thwart or progress the quality of life of others (2 Cor. 13:5–8; Rom. 14:12–13). Your silence or your statement of yes or no to any or all outlined may play a part toward your next level. Every phase in one's life has steps and measures to move from one level to another, both physiologically and spiritually. The two go hand in hand to enable individuals to develop attributes needed to handle success, tolerate others, obtain precise mission statements, and operate on them. Thus, your smooth transition to another level may depend on your performance at the previous level. If that be the case, it is imperative that you check mitigating factors against upward mobility. Embracing the future is a mere projectile of your present to the next, using harbored feelings, mindset, skills, and experiences—which, if there are flaws, will also affect your move.

We have patches in our lives from rubbing on others as they rob us. Negative words, criticisms, silence treatment, and mistakes of those in authority over us are a few examples of things that can create holes in our pockets. We may also have patches from hurts, past negative experiences, and unresolved issues. People, momentum, systems' policies, and situations will always change, but changing within yourself to accommodate these changes is your responsibility. Until you mend your ways to work around these sundry issues, your next level may be up in the sky for not being ready. Amid the hurdles of this life comes a list of worries caused by others. An example of this list is having a roommate who is not worried about paying his or her portion of the rent and utilities. Whereas the system does not recognize the faithful person when it comes to eviction proceeding and cutting off the utilities, the onus to keep the unit rests on the faithful. This is where wisdom and discernment in making choices play a role in becoming proactive. Being proactive is crucial because efforts to change the behaviors of people can be nerve-racking and challenging. However, studying God's manual provides benefits, wisdom, positive attitude, and discernment to make better choices (Luke 6:35).

Furthermore, God's net enables you to not only work on your character but to discern catastrophes far ahead of time, per His will (Eph. 3:16). Knowledge, creativity, innovation, integrity, and objectivity, as well as dealing with people and structural, physical, and financial challenges, are important factors in considering your next level. There can never be a better way to navigate against these mitigating factors than to partner with the life partner God Himself for resources, protection, help, guidance, and support, putting you on the sure path already mapped for you (Job 17:9; Ps. 27:5). Events of our modern times are signaling bold and writings on the walls to refrain from doing things in the old ways. For doubters, the systems, gadgets, industries, and services are all going electronic, signaling a new phase. Thus your next level may be gloomy if you fail to check the company you are keeping for verification of upward mobility. Being surrounded by forward thinkers, people who respect others and God's authority have never been paramount; there are always resistors in every good move for alertness. People are the center of every plan that God has for all creations. Thus any expectation, company, prospect, and hangout that does not contribute positively to the growth and development of people, stay in the cloud, for lacking visibility and viability.

Your next level is guaranteed no matter your setbacks, when you devote your life to serving, thinking, and helping others realize their dreams. Your vision to expand your scope for the purpose of making a positive difference comes from God, the writer of mission statements. His mission statement is written with precision for each of us to become the feet, hands, eyes, voice, ears, and heart of others (Jer. 1:4–10). Thus your next level is dependent on aligning your mission to become any and all of the above to others. There is no mission that is impossible when you network with God. His mission statement is very specific, simple, thorough, and carefully written as to whom you should serve, relate, when, and how, with appropriate links to others. People will fail to reach their next level according to God's plan when they draft their own ideas as mission statements for gain and pomposity. People are God's heartbeat; as such, He will never allow any cloudy, vague vision, no scope or mission-driven plan of anyone, to ruin His creations. Who is the author of your mission statement? It will always have a hidden ulterior motive if it does not come from God. In this regard, your next higher level may become an impossible mission. However, God's mission statement leads to missions being possible, transitioning from one level to the next (Phil. 4:13).

Your migration to the next level begins with stepping out of your comfort zones in response to the needs of others.

Staying On Course for Bigger Dreams to Enable Others to Realize Their Dreams

Staying on course has never been so crucial. We face changes in technology, structure, and methodology. Every aspect of life has been affected by both technological and economical structures. However, you always have an in-house mentor or coach to help you navigate. Most people do not know their destinies and are bent on doing their own thing, without the master plan. Do you know that you are just a tiny drop of water that could evaporate when you refuse to connect to form the big pool required for navigation? A teachable heart is necessary to receive instructions from the helper, the author of the master plan. The best athletes and movie stars stick to the master plan of their coaches. It is very evident that the best quarterback is helpless without a coach. Thus, as our world goes through various changes, it is crucial to stay connected to the coach, mentor, and helper to embrace the future (Prov. 3:11–26). The indwelling spirit of God in you speaks all the time about staying on course, however your craving for things outside the master plan interferes with hearing Him. Life is full of obstacles to neglect this voice in our turbulent world. Most of the decisions that have landed many people in deep troubles may have resulted from not listening to this voice. Your closest friend is incapable of knowing how to offer help, but the inbuilt mentor knows those feelings that play significant roles when you invite Him. Each day has challenges to require comfort, as well as affirmation that you are capable of such situations to avoid giving up (Ps. 147:8–18).

The fact of the matter is that you cannot comprehend and integrate your plan to the master plan without the helper, and that helper is the Lord

(Ps. 121). Your victory is assured when you listen to His counsel. People try to blame God for not obtaining what is rightfully theirs. Can you give a car key to your young child who does not have a driving license? The maturity needed to obtain your treasure is verified by the helper that knows your actions and words. He is very willing to coach you with the slightest inclination. The sooner you sign up, the better your chance of obtaining the resources, domain, and connections needed to fulfill purpose. The ultimate plan of the master is to use your talents and wisdom to coach others. The willingness to do so provides added knowledge, fulfillment, and progressing growth of people you have touched. Your best in action will always produce the best in others to be their best. The best part of your sacrifices is having voices that echo far into the future as the people you have touched experience break through to replicate for economic growth.

There is a broader purpose in life other than having a career and becoming successful. The Creator's plan is to aggregate each tiny droplet in each of us to form an ocean to navigate. An independent pursuit without proper integration of roles will always create a gap and no port for anyone to land. This is the very reason each institution has a master plan to steer, restructure, develop, and accommodate everyone in the team for advancement. The master plan is needed to structure your life; this calls for reviewing and renewing your plans to accommodate others, as they do the same. It is relatively impossible to think about others without the helper. Further, the same helper ensures the smooth sailing of your ship amid turbulent winds; without Him, you may not know where, how, and when to land. Historically, no one has ever calmed the wind except the master, who has the wisdom, direction, and information uniquely meant for you (Prov. 8:22–36). The active pursuit of things outside the master plan has its consequences, as per King Solomon. He was the most wealthy, talented, well-known, fun-seeking king that has ever lived. He cautioned anyone operating outside this master plan to retreat and avoid the consequences that it brings (Eccles. 2:1–11).

Finally, it is very amazing that the most designated caretakers of our world lack the wisdom and connectivity to stay on course. The ways of the ants have proved that connectivity and structure is inert in every creature. Ants obey, stay, and stick to the commands and structures for success despite various inclement weather. It can be inferably deduced that the complexity, ambiguity and various uncertainties experienced by mankind resulted when people tune off their receptors to do their own thing. It is time to simplify your plan, seeking feedback to amend ways using God's manual. Without this, you may land in the wrong port for hanging around a bad crowd or for being deceived by the many Delilahs out there (Judg. 16:4–21). Sampson was one of the strongest men, yet he succumbed to Delilah for doing his own thing. The same spirits exist today in the form of alcohol, drugs, and other tantalizers. Families, close circles, employment places, and religious institutions have important roles to play to ensure people do not fall victim, especially during hard times. One of the major reasons for people recoiling in their shells and not letting others know what they are going through is a lack of trust. The issue has come up again and again with the Sister to Sister group in Boston, Massachusetts and other affiliated groups. People should not be judgmental but be guided by empathy for not knowing the grassroots of issues faced by others. However, people will be won over if we all take time to uphold, appreciate, encourage, and incorporate others as valuable contributors in every communication, plan, and community development. It is not the time to be defensive but to safe-guard the self to stay on course for a happier and prosperous you.

A person whose mind is made up to help others is always inspired to study, thereby becoming a life learner needed for influence.

Strong Identity, Fearlessness, and Team Spirit Are Powerful Forces for a Meaningful Impact

If you do not know by now, the zesty, tasty aspect of life is derived from your determination to see opportunities in challenges and by wasting no time in harnessing all forces to prevail. Improvement, preventive measures, safety nets, adaptability, and a sense of self-worth are inside every creature (1 Pet. 5:10). However, God has endowed the tiniest of these creatures with super intelligence to steer you into actions that are limitless. Fear, laziness, lack of identity, trust, team spirit, and effective communication are just a few examples of things that have robbed most people from prospering (2 Cor. 5:17–21). The effectiveness of any corporate body is dependent on its strong identity, teamwork, dedication, performance, and flexibility in adapting to social, environmental, physical, technology and financial changes. This is faith at work, which is God's plan for mankind, also displayed by ants (Matt. 19:26). A strong corporate structure uses derived vision to harness all members into proper division of labor, whereby everyone sees each other as valuable contributors. The vision becomes the driving force that propels members to work jointly, obeying instructions regardless of physical location.

Every country that has succeeded in getting its independence has gone through making sacrifices, being courageous to harness forces to obtain its identity. Your realization that you are an image of God is your strong identity to see nothing as impossible when you know His will (Gen. 1:26; Ps. 8:5–8). The strong identity provides pertinent information about your freedom to refrain from enduring unnecessary hardship, pain, failures, diseases, and identity loss (John 19:30). The freedom comes with a new mindset as you study the manual of life, the Bible (Col. 1:15–21). It is a mindset of seeing yourself as God sees you: a winner, created to see the bigger picture and to retrack to achieve. It comes with a high level of trust in the Lord to persevere even in adversity, and to eventually obtain all His benefits. It is a mindset that gives you new ideas to become creative and improve continually. It is a mindset of willingness to change from within, as the Holy Spirit works on those grey areas that slow down your progress (2 Cor. 13:5).

The organized structure of ant colony is proof that you have what it takes to make it. The detailed structure is God's way of alerting mankind that He cares deeply about the minute details of your life (1 Cor. 1:27–29). It is very inferential that if God can give the tiny ants such super intelligence to run a corporate body, your imagination is much higher to run His empire (Luke 15:31). As Christ's ambassador, you are equipped to utilize everything on the planet to produce to the max, being careful not to destroy the lives and things you are meant to build (2 Cor. 5:20). The following ant ethics are valuable lessons worth emulating for success. Ants have an organized, integral structure with functionality that is intertwined in the division of labor. Ants move, work, and fight together to achieve common, mutual goals. A soldier ant is not reminded to step out of its sentry zone to respond to an emergency and to return back to the original post upon completion. Ants have a strong sense of identity; a mason ant is not intimidated by a soldier ant because of its strong belief that no one will take what is willfully his or hers (1 Sam. 9:23–24). Ants have great adaptive skills to a changing environment and are not intimidated by the size of any object, including human beings. Ants are fearless with their made up minds to continue on their mission no matter how one tries to interrupt. The mentality of each ant is programmed to obey the chain of command, focusing on the task ahead and ignoring all external forces. They understand teamwork, mutual trust, and effective communication.

The strong identity inference from the ants shows that your identity is your trademark to be reckoned with, to attract people to network and relate to you at all levels. It is who you are—your character, dedication to duty, integrity, scope, and faith—that manifested for submitting to the tiny, still small voice inside of you. You will gradually acquire new values and profitable attributes like the ants with God's words. Ants are able to work relentlessly, stopping at nothing to accomplish established goals because of their obedience to the chain of command. God's will for your life gives you strong identity, boldness, organized life, peace, adaptability, fearlessness, meaningful information, and effective communication via wisdom. Isn't it mind-boggling that ants in each colony respond to the same instructions regardless of their numbers? Your inner mind will respond to issues, circumstances, and more in your orchestrated network, regardless of your physical location, for your well-being (2 Tim. 1:13). If nothing is happening in your life, take time to study the ways of the ants for persistence, boldness, purpose, goal-oriented lifestyle, dedication, and focus for prosperity.

Co-integration of talents, skills and experiences form a unified identity as members lower their hats for others with better ideas,

Super-Sizing Your Impact during Crises

A closer look at our world shows unprecedented challenges, from financial crunches to global warming, that could cloud an outlook of anyone without hope. It is also expected that there will be more critics during austere times than problem solvers (Num 11: 1-15). Complex problems, negative outcomes of what used to work before, and major losses are sure signs of a quantum shift to the next level. It also requires positive mindsets and people from diverse walks of life working toward solutions. Super-failure in super places is a sure sign that there may be gaps, holes, accommodation issues, and loss-to-income imbalance. It also a positive sign that the best minds from diverse populations need to work together to support noble leaders in diverse places for solutions. It may be a sign that those rated "super" need reorientation and that leaders are servants to stoop to the levels of those served for tips. The "supers" lose every day, failing to reach the target population. We are all affected by family background and the earlier orientation it introduces to our lives. Some people's initial orientation may have been plagued with drugs, alcohol, abuse, and discouragement.

Time and time again, we are reminded that having a clean house requires cleaning some messes. We are all blessed with the Creator who, because of the coming of Christ, has provided us grace to things done out of ignorance. Thus as we celebrate the season of giving, spending time with families and decorating our environment, let us not fail to give a special salute to Jesus Christ, who came to raise the bar again to the failed strategies of mankind by displaying those attributes written in the Bible. The manuscript was written to provide examples of how we should serve others to be celebrated. It is written to provide solutions for comfort, acceptance, safety, and accommodation. The most interesting thing is that God came down to our level to prove to you that you matter so much; no matter how beaten, ostracized, defeated, and shamed you feel, you are made in His image. How else could He feel your pain, imprisonment, and neglect, without going through same Himself? The question now is where do you go from here? Would you let past mistakes, downsizing, a failed marriage or business, and relationships prevent you from living a celebrated life? The reason for the season is to provide directions for a better future for you. It is a season of good news that no matter your situation or predicament, you have a second chance to make a U-turn for the better. The season is also alerting you that you are well equipped through the Holy Spirit within you. Accept Christ to lose every intertwined factor weighing you down.

Being targeted for oppression, suffering, pain, and more may be a sure sign that you have great potential to take on hidden treasures. You must remind yourself that robbers target profitable ventures like banks, treasures, and potentially great people. Fight every doubt, denier, and skeptic so that you can have a great future. Accepting the message of hope—that every painful experience is meant for your gain—is the truth and factual for Christ to go through same. The message is an act of faith that believing in Christ provides. Faith comes by hearing God's words to obtain His promises and benefits. This faith cannot come through any other way except through Christ and God's words. This door cannot be super-sized by any other door, with proof from history of the failures of fake doors. Allowing thieves to rob you of your benefits, joy, dreams, and destiny is a personal choice that lacking knowledge of His words brings. The knowledge of His words cannot be compared to any technical knowledge; rather, He deposits talents in children as gifts to develop the world (Ephes. 2:8–10). Your joy will be full this season with the realization that God loves you so dearly. The absence of Christ is a super-failure in whatever you do, no matter how you to try to super-size the solution. The knowledge of God's words provides insight and understanding of supernatural things so that you can become a super-solution. The divine will, purpose, plan, and insight about spiritual things become clear when we study God's words to develop faith and to obtain the wisdom to live purposefully.

Maximizing the use of positive impact is a brilliant plan for victory in challenging times.

The Skill Set of Knowledge, Impact and Technology are Your Seeds for the Future

In this age of increasing technology and regulatory standards, finding the right mix of people to handle changes can be very challenging. Most businesses are trying to find ways to manage a myriad of issues at low cost. More often than not, one-stop, off-site approaches may be unable to address regulatory, compliance, and other one-to-one troubleshooting issues. It is evident that online transactions and self-checks are here to stay, and so are the skill sets needed to address those issues. It is also expected that because of technology, there will be more federal, state, and agency standards to safeguard entities and the people. The good news is that another level of manpower is needed to take care of targeted issues—new job opportunities. Thus, skill sets, experiences and knowledge of information technology are crucial to secure jobs in the future (Prov. 9:8–9). There are no two ways about it: high-tech issues are here to stay. It is very clear that the right combination of skills, special certification, and problem-oriented models is an emerging category of workers.

This combination requires grass-roots, problem-solving individuals already specialized to handle specific elements of performance issues. Our world has been transformed into a new era that requires handling various executive orders and guidelines that unfold each day because of technology. This focused, targeted approach is very effective in tackling improvement and compliance initiatives in healthcare, pharmaceutical, and human-service systems; it calls for skilled people with focus training to address problems and new areas for compliance for cost containment and in-house training by super-users. It may take only an e-seminar or refresher courses targeting specific issues to satisfy requirements (Prov. 8:18–21). An integration of skill sets, careers, and technology is a way for you to go if you want to move to the next level. A careful review of your profile is needed to determine areas of weakness. Filling the skill gaps all the time is God's plan for the world (Prov. 2:6). A careful look at God's creation shows a calculated, precise, architectural, structural, topographical, and unfolding informational set that beats every new technology. God is very precise and problem solving–oriented for you to imitate His image.

The cutting edge of information technology, even though it provides data at a snap of a finger via websites and social media, has risks and uncertainties. Managing the changing applications poses problems for every entity and certain populations to require new categories of workforce to help others to navigate. The need to monitor the interface that pulls data from multisystem information exchange is another area of opportunity for ancillary workers. Further, the point-to-point targeting issues and services is a "just in time" approach to promote jobs with better outcome for less.

It is in God's plan for mankind to utilize an expert exchange approach to solve the problem of the world (Eccles. 5:19). God purposely puts each part of the body to serve a specific need. Who could manage IT infrastructure, security issues, and hidden keyholes from malware and malicious usage? At last, the Creator's voice is sounding louder to streamline, configure, block, and operate with caution. There is no approach that is new to God; He has already mapped all apps in His words for you to use (Prov. 8:22–36). Individuals and entities are responsible for coming up with measures to improve their relationships and quality of life as they address conflicts, friction, skill sets, problems, and the well-being of others. Utilizing gifted, experienced, and committed individuals in every aspect of our delivery system will surely address the needs of every entity. For example, a golf ball in the hands of a novice amounts to nothing compared to the millions of dollars it will generate in the hands of Tiger Woods.

The new age calls for specific, targeted problem-solving for placement, promotion, and finding jobs. This approach will not only help you to occupy your domain but also enable you to accommodate changing needs to prosper. The Creator's web call is current, productive, prosperous, and available twenty-four seven (Eph. 24:25–32). You will do yourself good by blocking your ears and eyes from those apps that do not promote or add value to your life. The wisdom derived from His manual enables you to see your endpoint and go for it. You will learn to watch your dialogue portals, for out of them come either promotion or demotion (Prov. 18:21; Matt.

12:37). You will also learn to delete negative thoughts before they become actions that may affect the use of your talents to positively impact others. The failure to know when to switch off negative thoughts can affect your purpose and fulfillment.

Trading your stand alone territorial culture is a great move towards broadening your horizon.

The World Is In Need Of People That Never Give Up

Show me a person who has never quit in life, and I will show you a winner. The spirit of not giving up needs reinforcement because of its importance for development, stability, and growth (Rev. 3:11, 21). Persistence is the key to obtaining what you are looking for by working long enough to obtain it. It is the key to finding a solution to any problem by studying and analyzing them for solutions. It is the key to discovering the good side of others by taking time to relate to them. The attitude of not giving up is one of the characteristics of a person who's convinced that his or her pursuit has a victorious ending. A persistent person has patience, which is very essential in most homes to reduce the rate of people walking out on each other. By God's design, family members are meant to have close ties as a result of enhancing each other's good qualities and reducing the bad. Patience is a sign of trust in God for all your problems (Ps. 55:22); it is a faith in action, waiting patiently with a belief that delay is not a denial. People do not receive their heart's desires by not waiting long enough to receive direction, develop necessary character, and obtain special skills for their assignments (Exod. 2:10–15). Jacob was one of those men with a persistent personality who had to work for fourteen years just to marry the person he loved. He used the same spirit to wrestle the angel all night and to receive his blessing. The persistence of Jacob gave birth to a new nation, Israel (Gen. 32:24–30).

Your persistence in prayer is capable of changing every negative situation to a positive one at your home, at your place of work, and in society. It is in God's will to have stability at home, but you have to desire peace and stability to pursue them earnestly (Ps. 34:14). Children are precious gifts from God that require patience and firmness. It is not in God's plan that His gifts for mankind be twisted, misinformed, ruined, and unpurposeful. Parental patience is therefore required to discover and nurture these gifts. Patience is a sign of spiritual maturity developed by relating to God to want to do His will (Col. 3:1). Persistence is a testament that you are seeing things through God's eyes by embracing life one day at a time (Matt. 6:26). For example, you're tempted to change careers, churches, and relationships as often as your flesh desires when you lack God's direction. Persistence and patience work together in the life of a faithful person to enable him or her to stay long enough to rise up after a fall (Isa. 49:15–23). It provides you with enough time to learn valuable lessons and to quit making the same mistakes (Rev. 2:19).

Could you imagine the state of our world if there was retaliation for every offence? Our world will be full of offended people attacking and outdoing each other. It takes patience and spiritual maturity to stay calm every time people going through various challenges offend you. It takes patience not to send one of your family members out of the house for misbehaving (Prov. 25:28). Patience has paid off for those employees who have climbed up the ladder in their jobs. Dedication, paying attention to details, and being loyal are important characteristics that can move anyone from the bottom to a great height. Doing little things at your best has the propensity to attract those in authority to promote you (1 Sam. 17:40–50).

A non-quitter is determined to impact his or her environment and to not let the flaws, blind spots, and grey areas of others affect him or her. Quitters do not stay long enough to obtain the root causes of issues or to not solve them for rewards. The problem you are able to solve makes you a relative authority in that area. A non-quitter studies things, people, and situations for improvement regardless of how long it takes. It takes time to study others and to discover their strengths. You could miss important information by not taking time to listen, study, and analyze them; similarly, you could miss the voice and promises of God by not taking time to study God's words. Your miracle comes by faith, which is developed by hearing God's words. There is God's word for every challenge you could possible face in life. However, it takes a non-quitter to dig out these words and apply them to situations as they arise

Finally, God does not give up on anyone, so do not give up on yourself. He is actively molding, reshaping, and transforming you into that champion He sees (Matt. 28:20). Your flaws, imperfections, weaknesses, and inadequacies do not discourage God from loving you. However, it is important that you take time to study and obey His words to become that person of influence. This requires patience, persistence, and a fighting spirit.

Your recyled problems and negative experiences become the fertilizer to increase your domain.

Transformation and Reformation as You Walk into Victory in Hard Times

The rapid changing from how things used to be is not new, but a paradigm shift is occurring to change culture, doing more with less, as you collaborate to solve the problems of your environment. Staying rigid and uninvolved, without using benchmarks to plan, may not benefit you in our fast-paced environment. You are created to learn and relearn, focusing on the things you do best. The availability of modern technology has stepped up being your best in alignment with everyone's original job description. Technology has enabled anyone willing to learn to perform at their max. However, cost and manpower are huge factors for anyone to obtain all applications and to network with others in the same field. Our fast-paced, online-driven environment is a paradigm shift to be task specific and problem oriented, using available information to become innovative, creative, analytical, and target-specific. It is an exciting era of having informational work to prepare ahead in whatever you do. Timeliness in obtaining vital statistics, outcome measures, and success stories are positive forces to motivate anyone to plan ahead in this era (Prov. 14:8).

The new cutting edge is about providing front-liners with vital information to deliver noble services (Prov. 9:9). We are all here to serve for reward and fulfillment. Front-liners are usually those who know how to multiply, subdue, and increase, going into the deep for facts as caretakers. Are you surprised that God identifies with front-liners? Being a front-liner is title given to mankind in the Garden of Eden (Gen. 1:28). David was promoted by God caring for his father's sheep in the field as a front-liner, and he prepped for kingship. The time has passed whereby leaders and those in authorities hurl information to keep people, workforce, and associates in the dark. There is so much raw data out there for use to become a front-liner. God has already made you a front-liner, but to become one is your choice. A cultural change of relying on data governance to make the right choices is now available in our performance-driven structure. Front-liners are dependent upon others to provide vital information needed at work, home, and institutions of learning to make quality decisions. Front-liners, performers, and hands-on individuals drive every institution; they bring success, victory, and reformation where ever they go. Some of these people are transformed by painful and difficult circumstances to make a difference, taking seriously their assignments to preserve, persevere, and reform their environment (Prov. 1:5).

Transformation begins with the willingness to use everything that life, nature, and people bring to change, to do your best for the benefit of others. Successful people learn from mistakes, misfortunes, criticism, and sentinel events, having understood that failures can become prerequisites for the next level. Everyone's mission statement is to multiply, increase, and replenish the earth. Have you reviewed yours for focus, compliance, and outcome lately? Nonetheless, we have all fallen short as humans to change culture, habits, and character, and to also use, mistakes and tragedies for transformation and then reform our environment. The high cost of living and deprivation can have their ways of bringing creativity and exploration for better alternatives. A typical example of how a degrading, painful, and depriving experience could transform into reform is the story of a prodigal son (Luke 15:11–24). This rich, young adult blew his inherited money and ended up eating in the Dumpster with pigs. Losing the privileges as a destitute enabled him to appreciate the privileges he once had—and to go back. Most of us are in this predicament for not knowing what we have and who we are.

It is not the time to say that things are not working. It is time to be motivated, seeing yourself as a victor and not a victim, and to change the outlook. Following every wind of doctrine for not having a solid foundation, will earn you a whirlwind (Hos. 8:7). A whirlwind is known to blow away anything in its path. Aligning with God's will is your protection against such as you stick to your purpose, nurturing your environment for prosperity and recovery. There are many opportunities to turn things around. Changing outlook, attitude, character, paradigm, location, and domain are all God's plan to motivate people to make an impact. Burdens, compassion, patience, and focus are derived from transforming events to become change agents. Technology has provided these opportunities via collaborative and social media that provide success stories, insight, and templates for you to mirror. Our fast-paced world demands that you capitalize on technology to learn from the best and to be your best, using mistakes, pain, failures, and deprivation as fertilizer for the harvest (Prov. 24:16).

New employment opportunities come by deployment as you encroach on abandoned and neglected territories.

Triumphant Opportunities Result When You Reach Out for Others

There is always an entry and an exit door to a home and in life. However, there is something phenomenal about an entry door when it comes to being born, getting a new job, getting married, gaining admission to a school, and getting a new place to live. On the other hand, there is nothing exciting about leaving a job, marriage, school, and your home due to downsizing, divorce, being expelled, and eviction. There is also nothing exciting about exiting the earth, no matter how old or how prepared spiritually you are (Mark 14:36). But there is something good about triumphant entry, as displayed by God through Christ on Palm Sunday (Matt. 21:5–13). Every triumphant door has behind-the-scenes preparations. This is because every triumphant entry is preceded with turning the tables, getting rid of old and corrupt rituals and the things and habits you have knowingly and unknowingly exchanged for happiness. These are things you have held on to at all cost in place of God. God is very mindful of you and will not leave you without His intervention (John 14:18–21).

Everyone has held on to certain rituals, traditions, and lifestyles because of one's place of origin. Some convictions could be so strong that some culprits may feel they are doing God and society a favor (Matt. 21:12). It is very easy to lose focus and insight without guidelines and objective interpretations of the truth. Thus, the pathfinder Himself was sent on a mission to uproot all the rudiments of false exchange to create room for God's people to relate to Him (Col. 4:6). Prayer has been in existence since creation. Prayers and studying God's words are the most effective entry doors to establish a dialogue with God. Without Him, you will do your own thing and become alienated, distracted, and far removed from the very purpose for which you are created. Secondly, listening and learning from God will protect you from dubious buyers and sellers in our supplicated world (John 16:13). Some traditional rituals may have originated from the negative past with no meaningful use to our world today (Mark 3:1–5).

The question to you is, what are these traditional and routine rituals preventing you from listening and learning from God? A citizen of any nation can do anything to listen and learn from the president. God is more than all the presidents dead and alive put together, yet some people do not want to talk to Him because of misinformation and preoccupation with material and monetary exchanges. God created you to be triumphant. A renewed mind void of greed and zealous preoccupation will become triumphant. Jesus Christ is a very good shepherd who is deeply concerned about His sheep. There is a triumphant entry to places for anyone willing to feed His sheep on earth; this entails feeding others with pertinent information and services, to add values to lives. You carry this triumphant entry as a favor as you go about your business. Living triumphantly not only brings joy but also strengthens and lengthens your years on planet earth. Exchanging this triumphant lifestyle with greed and popularity, stepping on others, will always bring unhappiness (Matt. 6:19–21). Without a relationship with God, your likelihood to depend on others, money, and material things for affluence becomes very high. Your dependence on people and material things can be addictive for them to control you. The tendency to run into legal, health, and social issues is also high without God.

The same way good parents leave inheritance for their children, so does God leave it for us (Luke 11:13). He has given you every tool, gift, promise, and word for use to obtain your inheritance. God gave His best to the world as a ransom (John 3:16). The parable of the prodigal son painted a picture of God looking out for a rebellious child to return home to claim his inheritance. He was kneeling down while the son was standing up as they dialogued upon his return (Luke 15:10–24). This is quite contrary to the picture people paint about God. He is still pleading to you through His words and the Holy Spirit to build up faith for use to address every situation. There is God's word for every situation. Every one of God's words will come to fruition when you believe (Phil. 4:19). You were His body before the fall of Adam and Eve, and you are still His body when you believe in Jesus Christ now; the relationship has been restored again (Heb. 10:10–18). This was why Christ was furious with the sellers and buyers defiling the temple. You are God's temple to reciprocate through constant dialogues and obedience. Prayerlessness and blatantly ignoring the Holy Spirit may lead you to tarnish that image. Jesus Christ has turned the tables upside down for you, providing you with words to chase your adversaries. Your only part is to believe and obtain grace to enter triumphantly to places purposefully, giving back to others in love. You will then have continuous refills from heaven.

Simply having a talent does not guarantee that it will be put to good use to benefit you and others. This is where being reminded by positive thinkers, reading the blueprint of life (the Bible), and your realization that you are operating in obsolete can help you to plug in for reengineering. The rapid changes whereby the latest models of everything unfold each year is a notch to study the needs around you to plan ahead and to meet them. The needs of people will always be the economy and services. Society will always rely on people with extensive knowledge and skills to spearhead innovation and inventions. Thus those with useful information become the front runners to triumph in providing solutions to problems. Through optimistic visions of those bent on making an impact, people receive better quality of life in healthcare, as well as pertinent educational upgrades to match rapidly changing technology and networked environments to coordinate activities among different specialties. There is no question that people who seek knowledge, studying the needs and best practices to solve the problems of their environment, emerge triumphantly as winners.

The measure of success is not the amount of money that passed through your hands, but on how you extend your hands to others to experience success.

Turning Your Mess into a Message for Others

Do you know that the mess in your life could be recycled to reform you to multiply? Do you know that fertilizers, formed by rotten waste you threw in the Dumpsters, are used as boost and to multiply produce? The mess and challenges of life that manifested as your tears, sweat, past mistakes, and pain and suffering are your fertilizers for your use to sow seeds for increase. How? The valuable lessons have a way of transforming a selfish person into one who seeks others' interest. Seeking others' interest provides you the opportunity to receive abundantly from God (Matt. 6:33). The people are God's kingdom on earth (Matt. 6:10). Your mess has a way of making you see others as works in progress, and you should empathize, encourage, and help in their problematic stage to recover. Visiting those in prisons, hospitals, and homeless shelters, and those going through challenges by family members, are noble services to uplift people in this phase (Matt. 25:34–40). Every seed needs manure to boost it. Similarly, you have a seed as your talent that needs a boost. Manure from you provides the best boost. The best manure specifically needed by you to grow must come from you. Your uniqueness, special needs, and desired results are met through recycled wastes from none other but you. This is the reason skins are harvested from another part of one's body to treat burns and skin loss, for a perfect match.

Your mess has a way of creating a desire to help those who are presently in similar situations. For example, movies, texts, and inspirational books have been written by those telling their true life stories to educate others. Various programs have also emerged from charitable organizations to address special needs. Life is a phase; most often, it takes facing various challenges to get rid of the negatives to become better, productive, and enthusiastic. Life will become very boring and meaningless without some mess to work on to result in your helping others. However, you need some fertilizer of life to grow first. You cannot give what you do not have—fertilizer does not come any other way but from your piles of rubbish. Thus your own mess is a valuable source to create auto-fertilizers. The importance of fertilizer in your life can be verified by comparing two products of seeds planted with and without a fertilizer. The one without fertilizer will not produce to the max. So is the life of a person who refuses to recycle his or her mess—he or she struggles to create a fertilizer to boost his or her talent.

Remember, God has given everyone a seed as talent to sow on earth (Matt. 25:14–30). Your inability to realize you have a seed, and using your daily challenges as a learning curve to rebuild, will affect the result you get in life (Luke 13:6–9). Discovering your talent (the very thing you do at your best with ease) and your willingness to use people God puts in your path work together to map out your domain for maximum output. This is because you are building yourself to build others. You build others when you take time in your routines to help colleagues perform better. You build others when you encourage individuals facing challenges to hope again by offering physical, professional, financial, and emotional help as necessary. This is where the wisdom and life lessons of good retirees, veterans, long-standing employees, and married people could provide counsel to others coming on board.

The mess in your life brings out that sacrificial aspect of you to relate to God. God is sacrificial (John 3:16); a sacrificial person has the mind of Christ needed to turn around whatever is not working (Rom. 12:12). A sacrificial person digs into the trash for rejects, the neglected, and the forgotten in search of treasures with a mindset that God is still in the business of waste management (Mark 8:8). Such a person speaks to the problems as God spoke everything into existence. Further, whatever you make happen to others, God will make happen to you (Gen. 1:3–5). Most families are flourishing today because of a previous display of patience, kindness, love, forgiveness, and giving that someone has sown. Hostility, quarrelling, envy, jealousy, outbursts of anger, selfish ambition, division, and the feeling that you are always right and everybody else is wrong are life clutters to be dumped (Gal. 5:16–25). These clutters need a gradual dumping into the recycle bin as you renew your mind in Christ. The clutter is usually things that well-meaning people complain about you. Thus you should take advantage of God's waste management principle to recycle your pain, suffering, isolated situations, failures, and past mistakes for love, joy, peace, patience, kindness, goodness, self-control, faith, and gentleness to impact others for your wealth, fulfilled life, and happiness (Rom. 5:3–5).

Your performances improve via your mistakes and using such as learning curves to teach others.

Using a Lean Approach to Impact One's Surroundings

History has shown that victorious people are creative, innovative, accountable, and versatile, using every fat-trimming measure to prosper in season and out of season (Isa. 48:10–15). It is a special gift to micromanage resources to accomplish what needs to be done on a daily basis. Oftentimes it is not the amount of money given to a person that results in a desired product, but the ability of the person to apply wisdom, trim the fat, and engage the right people. This special attribute is important for improvement and development to necessitate those with it to teach others. Replenishing the earth by godly principles entails using a lean approach to run affairs of your life (Gen. 1:28). It may take a high cost of living in an austere economy for people to seek the Creator and to learn how to accomplish more with less. The Creator has been known to call out everything needed to sustain all creation by mere words (Gen. 1:3–11). You are His image, mandated to do likewise to sustain your environment with whatever you have at hand. However, many people do not know how to manage in hard times. It is also possible that people may not know how to become productive, even with great resources for relying on their own understanding of life. The lean approach to life has been God's plan for all: to not lean on their own understanding. Humility, patience, waste reduction, going after lost things and people, taking life one day at a time, being content with what you have, and watching what you eat and drink and say are all components of this lean approach. The lean approach has been ignored and neglected for lacking the knowledge of its importance to physical, financial, social reform, and economic recovery. A fast-paced environment has a way of making people develop fast-lane mentality to talk, eat, walk, and get rich quick with no time to actually relate to the self and others. The resulting effects are usually social isolation, health-related issues for eating poorly, and reduced incentive to explore home-grown technology because of an influx of imported goods.

The dwindling economy did not come as a surprise to God (Prov. 16:4); He has in the past allowed the situation to become so hopeless and then show up to restore hope(John 11:37–44). The current unfolding of events may be signals to dig into yourself, business, or career for redundancy, wasted time, and resources (Ps. 39:4) The inner spirit–driven aspect of you springs up at austere and critical times. The unique strategies, action plans, safety net, ingenuity, and power to formulate survival plans may stay dormant when people remain in their comfort zones. Oftentimes it takes losing everything that you thought has meaning to realize that you need God. History has shown that people who have aligned themselves with God's words, applying them to their situations, emerged victorious in the face of various challenges. These individuals are not only spiritual mature but have obtained faith to believe God at all times. You can never convince a person who fathered a child at the age of one hundred that God is faithful (Gen. 21:5). You can never convince a slave who became a prime minister in a foreign land that God is supreme (Gen. 41:39–43). The Bible is written for instruction, direction, and measures to follow, to convert every negative to a positive. Your unbelief in God's words will deprive you of joy and leave you panic-stricken in hard times.

Thinking cost containment and challenging yourself to weigh your options before making decisions have never been so critical. The hard economy has a way of changing our culture to think of ways to eliminate redundancies in whatever we do. Austerity provides people with the opportunity to test-run new ideas before making major changes. It provides people displaced job-wise or affected by a cash crunch to seek home remedies in handling problems and providing services. Home cooking and do-it-yourself improvement projects are common in hard times to improve health and fulfillment. There is always a derivable joy in accomplishment. You are joyful when you improvised and solved problems where you would have previously relied on professionals in prosperous times (Ps. 66:10–12). Painting, gardening, home cooking, and playing basketball in the yard with your children are examples of family programs with little investment and substantial gain. Spending quality time with your children will always leave an un-erasable mark in their footsteps as they walk this life.

The hard economy may be a sounding trumpet to improve our nutritional habit via home cooking, increased physical activity, and reduced TV time for a healthy and wealthy life. There are associations that study poor eating habits and heavy drinking: the Department of Agriculture and the National Institute on Alcohol Abuse. The Creator has a way of working everything out for the good to those He has called to do something in life. You are called to do something in life by being born and you should use cost containment and wellness to produce and have a quality life. The Bible has prescribed words, full of remedies on how to not shorten your victorious path. It provides vision into the future with a healthy, lean, management pathway to enjoy life. God's healthcare reform and economic recovery is the best, especially from the Creator and a friend that sticks so close, in season and out of season. Learning does not end when you graduate in any field; everybody needs to learn to become more prepared to handle challenges of the future. God understands this more than you to never call qualified people for any task (Matt. 4:18–22). He calls and qualifies through a painful, challenging process for upward mobility, gain, and victorious living that a lean approach brings (Matt. 10:1–15).

You should endeavor to teach those around you to cut their coats according to their sizes. Living within one's means is a joyful lifestyle that prevents individuals from vying for what others have, and from indulging in unwanted behaviors that could lead to complex problems. Thus, it is very beneficial to teach people around you to trim the fat in their spending habits and resource allocation. Parents should not borrow what they do not have to make impressions on their children; such a habit will lead to the disappointment when they cease, which may lead to the children seeking the same from deceptive outsiders. The lean approach to life is a power tool to impact your world; you should not be intimidated to use it.

The signs that things are not working, are redflags to change people and things around you for them to work.

Using Crises as a Pivotal Force for Vision and Impact

As illogical as it may sound, the real breakthrough of most nations, societies, and people come from major crises. The hidden gigantic strength—innovative ideas of unknown heroes—do spring up when people are hard pressed and terrorized by a huge issue. Absence of fear is often displayed by those divinely connected to God to intervene in these situations (1 Sam. 17:45–51). This is displayed when a father who cannot swim dives into a deep river to retrieve a drowning child. God did not give you a spirit of fear. Major storms, tsunamis, and other crises may not give you time to respond, but your faith in God will always attract His help to calm every storm. He will talk to your storms if you make Him your shepherd (Ps. 23:4). You have to be His sheep to hear His voice and develop your faith, acquired through His words. His voice, the still and small voice in your inner man, gives you direction on what tools, talents, and attributes are within your reach to fight back (Judg. 3:27–31; 5:1–6). The knowledge of God's words provides you with the instructions to overturn the overwhelming experience into an unforgettable deliverance. The un-erasable experience of the people of Israel at the Red Sea was a story told to every generation (Exod. 14:20–31). The valuable lesson here is that issues of life can pin you to the wall as an attempt to finish you, but your earnest cry to God for help will always attract Him. Every overwhelming situation can change for the best with God's help, when you value His relationship to help you value yourself to value His creation (Ps. 121; Isa. 45:2–3).

It is very obvious that a personal encounter with both positive and negative issues leaves us with lasting impression. For example, no amount of explanation can communicate the effects of war to a person who has never experienced one. It is for this reason that the storms of life of varied degree, size, and shape are inevitable and profitable (2 Sam. 22); it prompts you to have emergency plans for not knowing when and how the storm will hit. It entails your growing spiritually to diminish the flesh and to be able to overturn those complex issues of life that your natural strength is unable to address. Your body will always freeze or have a great shock with major storms; it can become too fearful with a minor storm to give up, depending upon others and engaging in unprofitable habits to appease the flesh. But your inner spirit is fighting back and takes over during severe, obscure situations. Institutions, nations, and individuals that thrive have disaster-preparation plans ahead of time. It is imperative that you tap into your built-in alert as a spirit-filled person to be able to handle life issues as they unfold. You are equipped as an image of God to survive the seasons to stay alive and to become progressive and productive. The flesh will always want to rule you to neglect your spiritual life, that part of you that hears from God. Your flesh cannot hear God. Spiritual maturity enables you to be watchful and purposeful, and to use whatever talent you have been given to become productive and influential. The Holy Spirit is your helper to guide you in every step of the way. Just like someone going on a journey, you need a pathfinder, peace, grace, direction, protection, and provision. Jesus Christ is all that.

Have you realized that you have no choice but to take risks when you are hard pressed? Storms have a way of moving you out of your comfort zone to places you wouldn't go. It gives you opportunities to step out in faith and be adventurous to advance. You have to advance and confront whatever is terrorizing you in order to gain freedom. Facing your storms gives you confidence and also prepares you for the next one. However, professional overconfidence, ignorance, and social pride can prevent a person from trying. Meeting the changing needs of others is one of the reasons God gave us varied talents.

Large storms have a way of enabling us to uncover, develop, and or rehabilitate these talents (1 Pet. 4:9–10). People may stay too long on former ideas and accomplishments when nothing moves them. People can become impatient with others who are less fortunate or are facing challenges. Major storms are melting pots, affecting everyone in its path. The prompting of the spirit of God inside of you enables you to use your accomplishments and talents to help, teach, and improve your environment (Prov. 18:16). God will give more to people who diligently use their talents to advance and impact lives; storms and other overwhelming emergencies can become great opportunities to do that. You will never question the existence of God when a bird provides food for you in a cave. The tsunamis and major storms of life have a way of making total strangers send aid in kindness and deeds across nations to break the dividing walls of religion, language, race, and socioeconomic status. God blesses any nation or person who extends a helping hands to others in times of need. This life is about sowing and reaping (2 Cor. 9:6–8). Rather than worrying about layoffs and other storms, engage your mind on how to use your smile, kindness, calmness, and encouragement to help others.

Challenges are propellers to the other profitable side yet unknown.

Virtualization: The Calling Out of a Hero in You

Virtualization is not a modern concept but is the fundamental principle of every creation. God virtualized the seas, mountains, nations, vegetations, animals, human beings, and more inside the void of earth (Gen. 1:1––12). He architecturally, technically, morphologically, and physiologically planned every creation ahead of time, before calling them all out one by one. To top it all, God deemed it necessary to have a family of His kind to not only continue in this creative path but to be the caretakers on earth (Gen. 1:26–30). It is only by His grace that your mind becomes receptive of His words, the same way He used words to bring illumination in your thoughts for creativity (Eph. 1:18–19). The miracle of virtualization before the physical manifestation has been in existence since creation, however mankind has failed to use it to the fullest to change negatives into positives. God has established this creative principle of allowing you to foresee, conceptualize, plan, and execute; it is a platform of problem solving to gain ground and become victorious. Entrepreneurs, IT vendors, and innovative thinkers are delving into this godly principle of creativity to address complex issues of our modern times (e.g., cost, accessibility, portability, flexibility, operational efficiency).

Many people are living defeated, deflated, and stagnated lives because of their lacking knowledge of this truth. Your failure, unhappiness, perpetual struggles, and vision loss may be the result of not applying this principle to become innovative. Innovation is simply a creative imagination in your mind's eye for solving problems, seeing finished products and endpoints ahead of time, believing wholeheartedly to pursue and obtain.

Every signal is pointing to a meaningful change of mindset to affect stagnant, unproductive situations and challenges using the same principle. The fact of the matter is that we are limited in our thoughts without God's grace. Most of us have lived long enough to know that our fleshy desires can become strong influences; no matter how hard we try, we need God's grace to break through (Rom. 8:12–16).

Be mindful that you need a renewed mindset to succeed (Prov. 23:7). Ignorance has plagued most of us to think that God wants to deter us from enjoying life or living happily (Hos. 4:6). He called us "mini gods," having made us in His image to create and recreate (Ps. 82:6). We have an imaginative mindset as children of the Most High. The reason most of us fail is that we have not taken time to imagine a thing, let alone plan to execute it. Most of us have not taken time to desire what we want in life or what we want to become. If God, as supreme, omnipotent, and omnipresent as He is, took time to carefully plan the world prior to execution, how come you think you can achieve anything without earnestly desiring, perceiving, and planning to execute it as well?

The affirmative outcome of virtualization to receive was displayed by Abraham to obtain his inheritance (Gen. 13:14–15). Another scenario played out when the tribe of Israel was about to occupy the Promised Land. The outcome of failing to see and not see things in your mind resulted whereby only the people who saw themselves as giant killers were able to enter the Promised Land. But those who saw themselves as grasshoppers in their mind never made it (Num. 13:30–33). In essence, seeing yourself as defeated in your mind can result in living a defeated life. Thus there is something phenomenal about developing a mindset of perceiving, conceptualizing, and believing. Your identification with the Creator is instrumental in acquiring all that in order to think good thoughts and focus on improving your environment as need be. Your fellowship with the Creator enables you fill your vocabulary with action words to effect changes; it equips your mind to have virtual images that will in turn develop into real pictures. Traditionally, spiritually and technically, you get a picture of what you focused on.

You will be surprised that the reason you have not gotten out of debt or obtained your breakthrough is because of your mentally distorted images. God has not placed any limitation on anyone, however your mind could limit and restrict you from possessing what is rightfully yours. The Bible is full of God's words and principles to not only guide you but to expose those grey areas that are standing in your way. The words give you the inner drive to expand your horizon amid obstacles, as well as conflicting and obstructing issues, because of your network. God's words make you creative, resourceful, and motivated as you see yourself as God's caretaker with a daily opportunity to impact the lives of others.

Your perspective about your surrounding affects your plan to either improve or neglect it.

Vital Information Is Important for Targeting Your Scope of Impact

Having reliable information in our changing world and adopting that information to reform your life is your key for advancement. Reliable information to counteract every storm, fight every fire, and withstand kingdoms on earth come from God's words (Rev. 19:11–13). The knowledge of God's words and using them will protect you from living a destructive and defeated life (Hos. 4:6). The most vital information you need to know is that you are created in the image of God to do something too big to handle, however you need details from God on how to proceed. You are also created by design to relate to God, who will in return show you how to relate to others. These two entities will satisfy your inert need to love and give love. Genuine love enables you to see others as co-contributors on earth to accomplish purposes, and to value and regard as important sources of your achievements. The feelings of not making a contribution and being unloved are known to make so many people unhappy. The cutting-edge information you need to know is that you are on earth to build healthy relationships and to make valuable contributions. You failure to do both will result in doing other things to fill in the blanks and in non-resolution of your problems. However, you can never do either of the two without having genuine love, which only comes from knowing God.

Knowing God enables you to see yourself as a royal, an image of God that can use every imagination in your heart to create things. Your lifestyle also changes as you adopt futuristic principles in dealing with people, situations, and the environment. A futurist looks into the future to visualize, document, and plan ahead for things to come through (Hab.

2:2–3). A futurist is not preoccupied with the present conditions (which are usually the opposite of developing plans), instead networking with others, and trusting God. For example, Abraham was quite old and frail, yet he focused on God's promise of having so many children that the prediction materialized. God has painted a picture of not looking at those who are presently misinformed, misguided, and full of mistakes but looking into their hearts, faith, and what He has deposited into them to give them amnesty (Luke 22:32). Your intentions, present information, and quest for the truth to turn around thereafter are in your heart. Abraham was a laid-back, ignorant man who turned around after knowing God to become wealthy and victorious (Gen. 12),which was possible because of his obedience and faith in God. His renewed mindset helped him to deal with his relationships and achievements, which are the most important elements of life.

The plan God has for you is usually too big for you to accomplish without Him. This is because you are created to relate and connect with Him to fulfill your relationships and goals. Most victorious men and women who had their big dreams and visions were obedient to God until fruition (Gen. 37:5–7; 45). God puts burdens on people to do something, which manifests in their lives as passions. Your passion comes with special grace and zeal; this is the reason people choose certain careers. Furthermore, the principle of being creative, tapping into the future, using our minds eyes to imagine solutions, and providing answers to issues are all in your genes, to do whatever God calls you to do (Gen. 11:6–8). God will allow you to put your faith into action as long as you don't become too overzealous and infringe on the plans He has for others. He may allow some disastrous human plans to materialize for outcomes and effects to teach others (Gen. 4:3–11). For example, Samson's power was given to him to fulfill a divine purpose, but he failed to abide by the principle of the truth to his shame, defeat, and destruction (Judg. 16). The tools, energy, and physical and spiritual attributes to perform your purposes are at your disposal. However, God still looks deep into your heart for intentions, obedience, and your ability to relate to Him and others. This is the reason why He intervened in certain situations that are mind-boggling to ordinary eyes. The hearts of people are usually hardened, and our lives are out of control for not knowing God and being guided by His principles. Royals and dignitaries are guided by principles for preservation, integrity, and security. God has called you a royal to be mindful of the treasures, authority, and inheritance you have, not to live, act, walk, and talk any way you wish.

You are created in God's image with the ability to put your imagination toward finding cures for diseases, and for providing solutions for problems and necessities of society in alignment with His will (Prov. 18:21). You have the power of visualization, planning, and execution. The mentality of having finished products on a silver platter is a sign of an unproductive life. God did not just wake up one day to call out the creation; He first thought them out, planned them; and then spent six days calling them out (Gen. 2:1–4). The fact of the matter is that you cannot achieve anything in life without tapping into the future to see ahead, making plans to execute them. God painted a picture of a void, a confused world that came alive for you to reciprocate. This requires a change in lifestyle, habits, plan, and principles obtainable in God's manual, the Bible, to do the same.

The sooner you realize what you do best at ease to apply meaningfully, the sooner your life will begin to have meaning.

We Are All Needy People to Impact Others and to Receive Impact

Traditionally, society looks down on people culturally termed the needy. This needy list may include the homeless, abandoned, chronically mental, and physical challenged. We tend to forget that we are all needy people, needing each other to fulfill our roles, destinies, and purposes on earth. The earth is a vast area to cultivate, subdue, replenish, and multiply by any one person; hence we need farmers, builders, developers, manufacturers, fathers, mothers, engineers, and more to keep our world running. Every created person has limited skills, and mental, social, physical, and spiritual capacities to handle life. We need God and others to be fruitful. Your clear understanding of this will humble you to treat people God puts in your path with respect, honor, and dignity, because you need them as they need you. Unity of purpose and better relationships emerge when people feel needed, recognized, appreciated, and included as team players and as image bearers. Every human is an image of God, irrespective of status, place of origin, language, gender, and color (Gen. 1:26).

The corporate principle of working together is critical and is emphasized in the triune whereby God the father, the Son, and the Holy Spirit work in harmony (Matt. 28:18–19). Christ sought the will of God the father, praying unceasingly to align his will, actions, and plans to His glory. God's authoritative head was respected at all time despite the fact that every creation was made by Christ, the Spoken Word (John 1:1–4). So is the Holy Spirit, the working power of God, that carried his role gently during creation as well as being the indwelling comforter to date (Gen. 1:2; John

14:16–17). As an image bearer, you are expected to reflect the submissive attribute for the effectual working to meet the needs of each other in love and humility. The constant reminder that you came from God is important to encourage you to think unity of purpose, service, and love in your daily dealings with people for peace and a prosperous life (Eph. 3:14–20). You are created to serve and be served as you mature physiologically, professionally, and spiritually as a child, worker, wife, husband, teacher, soldier, and more (1 John 3:1; Eph. 6:1–18, 4:11).

A child needs pertinent parental support for his or her next level. Children are the future work force, parents, and leaders, and they should be taught collaboration early in life. Homes are the first education depot to learn respect, service, and the importance of using the needs of others to choose career paths. Children are like sponges that absorb every action and spoken word of defeat, victory, fear, and faith. They may not be able to filter impurities and contaminants—this is the reason God cares about these tender-hearted children and deeply disapproves of those who abuse them (Matt. 18:6–7). A worker needs a place of employment to showcase his or her skills. Husbands and wives need each other to fulfill their purposes via support and complementation. A soldier needs a battlefield or security ventures to become a true marksman. Excessive display of pride and arrogance usually rules anyone who does not think he or she needs otherss to make it; pride goes before any fall. This is also the reason why God takes interest on the needy people per His words. The needs of most needy people were met by Christ as a display of how God identifies with heartfelt, needy people (Isa. 66:1–2). Needy people tend to persevere and are humble with persistence, trusting the Lord. Successful people are usually those who see the needs of others to become burdened to do what it takes to work on those needs. God is still using people with such burdens to continue His mission on earth.

People may construe being an image of God as an entitlement of power and enjoyment of God's creations, to the neglect of the spiritual aspect that relates to God. The exhaustive chase of things and people to fulfill biological and psychological needs may define your level of spiritual maturity. God is aware that you need food, housing, security, relationships, and networks, however the spiritual need is of absolute importance to wean you off from being selfish, controlling ,and caring solely about how to meet basic needs. The higher-level hierarchy of spiritual maturity comes with seeing yourself as a conduit to receive God's love and grace from Christ and to provide the same to those you encounter daily(Acts 1:8). This comes with great sacrifice of being an image bearer, working in the vineyard and serving others as He has served you. There is fulfillment, enthusiasm, satisfaction, and peace for the spiritually matured, for not being moved and moved by what others crave and have sleepless nights over (1 Cor. 14:15–17). It is the "seek the kingdom" phase that brings everything that you did not ask for you and your family for generation to come (Deut. 7:9). This is the good-news phase of helping others and serving your community as you realize your identity as an image bearer to receive from God with reciprocity.

Your kindness in enabling others to have their needs met, touches even the harden hearts to change and beat for others.

You Are Not the Mistake but a Noble Created for Noble Impact

This is a season of great awakening, delight, and honor in affirmation that you are a true replica of the Creator. You may not be able to understand the reason for some pain, afflictions, and certain happenings in your life; it may be also impossible to explain why good things happen to bad people and bad things happen to good people. One thing is obvious: you are wonderfully made to reflect God's image using all kinds of inadequacy, disabilities, pain, weaknesses, mistakes, and fragmented issues around you to bring miracles to others. Some interruptions in your life, even though they are painful, are there to redirect your course to glorious destiny (Luke 1:27–37). Some interruptions help you to develop discipline and burdens for others (Ps. 119:71). A person who listens to the soft voice within is able to understand that which may seem to be a mistake is for a season and good reason (Matt. 1:18–22). It is very obvious that people will focus on the mistakes of others, society, parents, and associates during hard times; making mistakes is very obvious in our broken and fragmented world. However, mistakes can be turned around, and failures can become triumphant entry doors to a celebrated life. This is the message of the season for those who believe.

This season is a story of a humble birth from a place mistaken to have produced nothing good. The miracle of the season came from a home mistaken to have produced nothing great. The receiver of the immaculate conception was a sixteen-year-old virgin mistaken to be naïve, yet she was full of faith to receive the spoken words from Angel Gabriel (Luke 1:26–37). Her torment, isolation, and ridicule reduce your issues to nothing when you think about her ordeal. Being offended, bruised, and rejected by people, especially when God has a great plan for you, is inevitable. The way you deal with what seems to be a mistake, pain, and detour determines your victory in life. Your joy is always full when you understand that the Creator is a restorer. The season is a reminder that Christ took every spiritual step to hand you back the keys of opportunities to increase and replenish the earth (Matt. 16:18–19). Everyone is affected by the aftermath of the fallen world; as such, there is no perfect person, home, job, society, or institution. There are all kinds of spiritual, physical, anatomical, and physiological deviations as a result of the fall—many corrective instructions have been given to mankind ever since, via the Mosaic laws and the prophets and angels, to no avail (Jer. 31:31–33). Thus the king had to come down from the throne to fix every broken area, once and for all.

This season marks the celebration of His royal visitation to our level for a better relationship and a closer touch. The Holy Spirit is provided twenty-four hours a day, seven days a week to protect, guide, and comfort you, just by your accepting Christ. The still, small voice enables you to sort out mistakes with the daily reading of God's manual to not miss opportunities designated to bring joy, wealth, and influence to your life. Everyone is capable of this grace, however your verbal consent is required to become a matured heir to the inheritance. We are all children of God, but not all His children are matured to handle the keys. The keys are only given to those who believe by accepting this special grace (1 John 5:1). It is very simple to verbalize the following: "I have accepted Jesus Christ as my Lord and Savior." Without this acceptance, we are all deflated in our character and are going nowhere with burdens, worries, and cravings for things that are known to be destructive. Alcohol, illicit drugs, and whatever else is used to numb pain cannot alleviate the frustration of a stagnated life. We are all members of Adam's family, prone to mistakes, hopelessness, and all kind of brokenness (Gen. 3:17–18; 4:9–12).

The roll of the dice of the season becomes real when others obtain the true essence of God via your willingness to use the cracks in your life to do good. There are valuable lessons to be learned by others when you are kind, patient, and full of encouraging words. This season empowers you to take back what has been stolen from you. It is a season of affirmation that mistakes could be turned around for benefits. The seed of turning things around is imbedded in your gene for meaningful use, to let others have their miracles through you. How? The way you handle difficult situations joyfully gives others hope without making a statement to impact them positively. This sharing comes from His love in all of us to give this season and more (Rom. 5:5).

The thought of self all the time may limit and isolate a person from deriving and making impact for fulfillment.

Your Bright Ideas Could Resolve the Key Challenges of Your World

You are created to define yourself by using events, issues, people, and your surroundings to birth ideas. Your mere observation of what is going on at home, work, and other areas provides opportunities for ideas to help situations and people around you. Ideas provide power, wealth, identity, and integrity (2 Chron. 1:11–12). You can never be bored when you seek to provide ideas on issues needing improvement. There are tons of issues, lessons, trends, frowns, and tears on people's faces, and solutions that your bright ideas could resolve to define you. People will define you with their limited timing and judgment. A good person having a bad day could be defined as a bad person by someone who had encountered him or her at that moment. Hence it is imperative that you do not let others define you, further burying your ideas. On the contrary, a phony person faking one-day celebrity in a rented limousine may have a swollen head by the remarks of people looking for favors—but he or she will fail to work on his or her buried talents.

Ideas are meant to help people to reduce stress, which comes from their willingness to see issues as unsolvable. Has it occurred to you that focusing on your problems too much has a tendency to wear you out? It depletes your joy to lack enthusiasm. Your joy is your strength. You are weakened by stress out of frustration of not being able to handle issues around you. Your noble idea is a form of releasing what is inside. The problems you are able to solve will promote you as others come to you for solutions to their problems. It is an act of giving out to mankind as you devote time to solve the problems of others. Reaching out to others and society with good ideas is a noble service of valuing your environment, investing your time, and cultivating those ideas. Your idea is an investment plan approved by God to grow people and His creations (Eph. 6:8). An idealistic person is full of expectations. Every spiritual and physical birth comes with expectancy. Your noble idea begins with a thought that transcends into an expectation with a conviction that it will materialize. This is your faith in action for invention, deliverance, progress, breakthrough, and blessings.

Ideas birthed by careful observation of one's surroundings meet the two most important principles for victorious living (1 John 3:17), which are having faith and a renewed thought process. As a person thinks, so is he or she. The way you think will define you at all season. In addition, faith is receiving answers to problems in your imagination to become fully expectant without reasonable doubt that they will come to fruition. It gives you hope and a sense of calmness to encourage, console, and support others in crises. Inventions, modern technologies, and improved quality of life are all products of bright ideas (Prov. 8:12). Your mind has wealth of ideas inputted by God for use to solve problems in your surroundings on a daily basis (Luke 6:38). The world we live in today calls for noble ideas to effect changes in our mindset, character, habit, and spiritual maturity to grow the environment. You are best qualified to come up with bright ideas on problems in your surroundings, having firsthand information unavailable to an outsider. An outsider who saw a community in its season of chaos may provide a wrong idea on how to help the people.

The world will be a better place if we all take time to observe issues needing attention, beginning at home; the aggregate ideas will then provide meaningful solutions for our world (Eccles. 4:9–12). Others will define your surroundings incorrectly for not being around in good and bad times. People will change sides on you depending on the season. A celebrity will have millions of fans in good times, with a drop in notoriety with a little scandal. You are an image of God with a wealth of ideas that can never be exhausted. You have to see yourself as possessing the solutions to the problems in your environment. The Rock was struck once to provide ever flowing rivers of ideas (1 Cor. 10:4; Exod. 17:6). The Rock is God's words, full of such ideas. These ideas are embedded in God's words, and when you obey them, they open doors of opportunities to define and prosper you. You are created to observe people around you in and out of seasons, and to birth noble ideas on how to solve their problems. Misery invades the life of a person with buried ideas within (Matt. 25:14–30). Ideas are meant to come out to benefit others, for the giver to reap the benefits. Ideas have the propensity to keep the mind active, worry-free, and rejuvenated as the participant involves others to create a healthy and wealthy society. You will joyfully delve into your valleys to look for ideas to better others, knowing full well that those defining moments will take you to the mountaintop.

Being burdened by the needs of others, enables one to re- arrange functionalities to have goals.

Your Interest Determines Your Impact

How you invest your attention, time, and money will determine your financial interest, fulfillment, and areas of influence and domain. God gives us simple and specific instructions to derive a rewarding interest (Matt. 6:33). People are God's interest. Your success, peace, joy, sustained wealth, and happiness is dependent on the value you place on people to invest in them. A carnal mind will use the law of borrowed money to buy material things for personal consumption, buying and selling for financial gain only. The love of money can make a person do anything to manipulate, hurt, extort, and destroy God's major interest—people. There is nothing wrong in acquiring riches as long as they are used to invest in people. God will increase your wealth a thousand times when you invest your money to help others experience God's love (Deut. 1:11). Every one of us has riches within us in the form of talent, to be used to touch people for long-lasting financial interest. The following interest guidelines are outlined below to help you identify and conquer your deficit areas: knowing the problems of people around you, and knowing God's words to see things from His viewpoint (e.g., a person's uncle died of pancreatic cancer, inspiring her to study for a cure). We now have a curative vaccine for pancreatic cancer when caught at an early stage. Embrace technology and family by providing adequate supervision of your children. Most parents take the easy way out, hugging their TV or watching news and sports websites, which inadvertently allows their children to do whatever they like. Join other interest champion groups in your job, children's school, churches, and social affiliations to address issues as they come for a prosperous you. Refrain from hiding behind religion, sectionalism, professionalism, gender, and cliques that deter you from being a good Samaritan.

The principle of sowing and reaping is God's kingdom formula for having the interest of others at heart in our daily choices. People are the only creation of God that can buy, appreciate, depreciate, and convey verbal or written approval of others. You have to sow abundantly by interest, investment, action, and services to reap overflow dividends (Eph. 6:8). Your overflow rewards come with vested interest of what people like or see in you to pay homage. Have you ever analyzed your interests and motives behind things you do in life? What are your vested interests in choosing your career, spouse, residential area, affiliation, and people with whom you associate? You have to work to eat and fend for your family, however you and your family should not be your primary focus. You will have enough for them with your earnest work ethics, but your overflow for reserve comes from your extended family of people. This makes your job not only a place to collect paychecks, but an opportunity to help others grow. People bring their pain, desperation, confusion, and issues to work. Your earnest attitude of being a colleague's keeper is a vested interest to help them achieve their potentials. We are all lacking from ignorance. Your encouragement, patience, information, support, and counseling are all areas of vested interest to touch others as you go about your routine (James 2:14).

The challenges of society are not the advent of technology, but people's desensitization of its access to abuse it. For example, the Internet is a good informational tool to help better people, however it can be used to exploit others. The growth of a society hinges on uniting people to plan, communicate, and team up with each other. There are rules and regulations adopted from biblical, ethical, legal standards to govern the lands, with expectations of doing the right thing upfront or paying for it later. There are expectations of transparency, deliverability, accountability, human relations, and outcomes with God and people. There is also an expectancy of risk avoidance with personal lifestyle, work ethics, and spiritual growth. This is because the images you portray will promote or demote you. Your desire to get money by all means, without caring for people, sends a red flag to people to query or detach from you (Prov. 22:22–23; 16; 23:5). It is very easy for anyone to fall victim to chasing money in order to satisfy their flesh, in absence of spiritual development.

This is where God's words come in handy to help you. Too many experts have a way of detaching from each other due to professional pride. The renewed interest in people will help you to see others as colleagues and to solicit and respect their contributions. You will not do things to jeopardize others when you are conscious of certain domino effects. You will not drink and drive to avoid injuring others. You will not be negligent in your line of duties whereby your errors may threaten others. You will discipline your children because their future contributions are important to the society. Your return on investment is guaranteed when everything you do has others' interests at heart. God fills up the tanks of life learners and life givers for their continual support of others. The Bible is the only tool that provides the directions on how to renew your interest and to get rid of selfishness, so you can invest in people (Ps. 112).

Your interest in people determines your dividend's interest as you take time to encourage and support others to soar to greater height.

Your Positive Impact Depends on Your Outlook

Your outlook about life does not only reflect your status quo, physical appearance, and achievements but also your link to others and the potter. Your outlook is always brighter when you sow seeds that challenge others to convert their talents into performances. Good seeds produce harvest for wealth and fulfillment; the principle of sowing and reaping cannot be broken, even when delayed. The seeds of love, kindness, forgiveness, encouragement, and patience have been known to create a phenomenal influence on people—more than money, given money's void of love. The people God puts in your path may remain in a state of hopelessness, poverty, or deprivation until you sow the right seed, per God's plan; the right seed produces a link to ignite the fading light. We are born competitors and are territorial in our Adamic nature to affect anything. In this state, you are driven by the spirit of acquiring more wealth and working harder to fulfill your fleshy desires (Gen. 30:37–43). The love of the potter is to keep you focused on the finish line designed for you (Phil. 3:13–15). This final design comes with joy, fulfillment, and people you have helped along the way.

Within the heart of a money monger, who is an angry, powerful, hopeless, fearful, and abusive person, is a need to be loved, touched, and reaffirmed that he or she is wonderful, beautiful, and purposely made. Oftentimes speed bumps are thrown here and there to slow people down and to get them to quit chasing the shadow (Gen. 32:11–30). Jacob was still holding on to the deception, doing things with his own strength and trickery, until he encountered the potter. He was then remade using his mistakes, desperation, and present scary outlook of facing his brother Esau to admit who he really was: the founder of the greatest nation on earth—Israel. God will always stop and listen to anyone who has come to the end of himself or herself. It takes a genuine brokenness to seek for a remake to really enjoy life. Jacob had everything, yet the mask of deception, insecurity, and fear was there to torment him. This outlook may be the fate of a person walking outside his destiny. A breakthrough is always imminent for a broken person with a genuine repentance, as God stops whatever He is doing to listen. He will move heaven and earth just to reach that person (Ps. 34:17–19). The lesson learned here is that you cannot save your face when are you seeking God to intervene. Mary Magdalene understood there was no face to save when she was at the very bottom and facing death via stoning, to change to her rescuer at all cost (Mark 14:3–9).

Your sole focus on your accomplishments alone, without linking to God and people, may prevent you to open up yourself for this beneficial remake. Without this link, you may be unprepared to handle the speed bump that life throws as you travel (1 Chron. 15:12–13). It is very easy to give up when fear, fatal losses, distress, and problems of the real world hit you. The winds of adversity blow on the poor, rich, good, and bad alike to reject the hope of assurance that the soothing voice of His spirit provides.

A shift in focus, powered by disappointments and things previously thought to bring joy, is the most effective driver of change for a better outlook. It is a total surrender of one's status quo and of not liking the present for something better. Everyone is not created with perfect looks, background, and supportive surroundings; there is no perfect environment free from setbacks, roadblocks, and limitations. However, reaching dead-ends, being knocked off the road by a speed bump, and eating in the pigpen via mistakes may be your chance to seek for a remake for the restoration of wealth, dignity, health, and relationships (Luke 15:11–32). You have to recognize that you have a crucial role: to let go the "ugly, hopeless, unprofitable outlook." After all, who will want to save the face of shame, dishonor, poverty, and bruises?

Seeking for a better future outlook, and still holding on to unprofitable habits just to save your face, is playing a game of deceit (Exod. 33:18–23). Simon Peter, the greatest skilled fisherman, reached that point of toiling all day without catching any fish to yield for a makeover (Luke 5:3–8). Peter had to let go his professional pride, surrendering to the dissenting voice, to experience the greatest catch. Your remake for giving up the old self has the propensity to visibly impact your surroundings. Your remake renews you for adventure. Live and succeed to impact others for aligning your will with the potter. Your new outlook will always bring fulfillment and joy, which flows from the inside to brighten your look and everything you touch, to the notice of others. Your social outlook via achievement may not create this link. Achievement and fame without good character could become your worst enemy as a result of affluence-related lifestyles—the wrong exchange of outlook for everything you have worked for. The key to operating in a better outlook is discovering your destiny for encountering the Creator.

How you see the future determines your vested interest in sowing the seeds for reciprocal harvest.

Using Even Your Painful Experiences To Enlarge Your Domain

As an aspiring, bright-idea thinker, you are responsible for using every painful experience that your background produced to increase more. The key to transforming negative experiences into positives is to first identify the root cause of your setback and then analyze why and how to avoid repetition. Such steps will become your boost to tackle problems. Making your pain or problem the primary focus of your existence paralyzes you in making the necessary connections and investments for impact. Answering your pain and wearing it as an outlook may become a stigma. Stigmas, achievements, and even great successes all have their ways of causing failure. The narrative of an Old Testament on the effect of wearing pain and how it was alleviated by the determination of the sufferer to replace this life-sapping dream killer with a life of purpose is a way to tackle any issue that plagues one's life. In this story, a man was named Jabez by his mother for suffering pain during the pregnancy and delivery; his name meant "pain." Everyone knew the meaning of his name and associated him with pain. This young man slept, ate, walked, and lived in pain. His story was a shackle and life pain remover for those stagnated by any kind of pain (1 Chron. 4:9–10).

We all experience various kinds of pain, however your life may be on hold when you become the pain, walking, working, and sleeping with it twenty-four hours a day and seven days a week. This kind of pain will not hit home unless, in the past or present, you have watched the torment of being denied. You should not expect people to give you credit as an honorable person in your painful and dark moments (Judg. 16).

Everyone knew that the young man was named Jabez by his mother, yet people associated him with bad luck, pain, and disaster, to torment him immensely. Thus, the labels people place on you can affect you when you are ignorant of using God's words to nullify them. You are to speak to the pain to receive blessings (Num. 20:3–8). Taking care of your pains in God's way brings deliverance, prosperity, and blessings to bless others.

Some pain may be very hard to treat because of the difficulty in locating the source. People have difficulty relating to God, the source, in their pain. The young man believed in the supreme God and asked for help to deal with the unbearable pain. The focus of Jabez's request was to remove his pain so as not to inflict it on others. He also requested for the enlargement of his territory to better others. Most of us would have asked for power to override their rivals. Anger, vengeance, and disobedience have prevented most people from receiving God's promises. The lesson here is that God is very interested in increasing your field, skill, and area of influence for use in bettering others. He is interested in people who nobly strive to remove derogatory labels that society, parents, and friends put on them. It is also a confirmation that God does not put such labels on any of His children. Thus, the petition to enlarge your territory and remove unwanted labels comes with an earnest request to the Creator. This can take place in your kitchen, prison cell, living room, homeless shelter, or anywhere else. God has given the responsibility of naming and caring for children to their parents; this task has been neglected, abused, and haphazardly done to blame God regarding how they turned out. Life, the environment, and people can put limitations on you, but living beyond those limitations is your call to make, to be celebrated.

Achievements and great success also have ways of causing failure. If you look around careful enough, you will notice that among the wounded and disillusioned dropouts of business and society and marriage, there are also famous people. This is because great achievements have a way of making people invisible, insensitive, and careless to ignore obvious warnings of doom (Judg. 16:18–21). Furthermore, pressure will always mount high for the famous as they try to keep up with their obligations. The resultant effect is having less time to do careful analysis and to grow spiritually. There are also many distractions as one climbs the corporate ladder to display the annoying attribute of pride of worshiping the blessings (1 Sam. 17:28). The need to watch for deception at the peak of stardom is a must. This is impossible without God, because no human is able to discern the minds of others. Everybody wants to identify with a successful person;

most deceptions come with friendly, harmless, and appealing conversations and with being persuaded by the deceived. The same baits used to catch animals are being used on people. No one is exempt from making mistakes and falling into deception.

Parents can make mistakes naming and raising their children. However, no one is a product of such mistakes because of God's grace; His grace is available for those that asked (Matt. 7:11). Peter was rescued from sinking by asking (Matt. 14:30–31). Jabez's territory was enlarged by asking; Jabez understood that God did not cause his pain. God is the "I am that I am." The way you see Him will affect your trust, relations, and your belief that He is able to do all things. He is very gracious and does not hold every bad you did against you. Moses was able to make it to the Promised Land by His grace (Matt. 17:1–3; Deut. 3:26). God's love, patience, and grace are beyond measure for people to refuse to simply ask for help not only to enlarge their territories but to keep them from trouble and temptations. Your catch area is your responsibility, for it is a known fact that many people have developed their passions through their pain. Some top healthcare specialists have chosen their career for developing the passion to solve the problems of others because their loved ones suffered from them. Nonetheless, God could also provide huge tasks for designated people requiring time, going through pain and great passion to develop them. For example, to become a United States Navy Seal requires rigorous and painful training. Thus, it is should dawn on people that pain is an integral part of life to strengthen, develop endurance, and firm one's purpose to better others.

Mankind is divinely made to turn every pain into gain with patience, informed knowledge and humility

Your Wealth Comes from Your Impact

Life has been simplified to use what you already have to impact others, just by taking responsibility and being accountable. Can you be trusted to perform as the need arises? Do you shun responsibility and break ties when things fail to go your way? The blueprint for victorious living recommends that you value others to appreciate, encourage, and establish trust to achieve common goals needed for prosperity. The people you devalued for refusing to do your part will never see you as a mentor or a person of influence (Gen. 31:5–7). It is also not by accident that a society springs up from homes to teach members to care, love, establish trust, and agree and disagree nobly. A home is a beginning point to learn to put heads together and to achieve common goals, show support, and develop the relationships needed to branch out and live purposefully(1 Tim. 5:4–8). A home with positive impact encourages members to migrate into leadership, noble career paths, entrepreneurship, and innovation, becoming developers of their world. The members of such homes learned through backup experiences to absorb shock and to hold on to their strong foundation in times of crises. Impact comes in various forms and sizes, often without warning. A person who impacts others will create new ramps as the need arises and will soar to great heights in life (Prov. 22:29).

Making an impact is the core to becoming successful in life. One's impact integrates a person into functional areas to become influential and a consultant. People in need always go to a person who has answers and who supports others no matter who and where (Gen. 40:9–14). A person desiring to make an impact should strive away from distractions, negative past, and hearsay. Refraining from these will enable a person to study the needs of others and to formulate plans for improvement. Time after time, the Creator has used His blueprint to spell out that making a positive impact is a qualifying attribute for a healthy and wealthy life (1 John 3:27). The common point in failing to achieve rests in people not adhering to this simple rule of valuing others and relationships. No one achieves anything by standing alone. By nature, people are afraid to make changes for the fear of losing grip on what is familiar in terms of character, habits, and whatever they are used to. Anything that involves process and cultural and habit changes create panic and resistance. In a nutshell, impacting others breaks any process and barrier stopping one from seeking to better the lives of others.

A strong impact is felt and is known to disintegrate, dismantle, and reshape the object of impact; so are phenomenal impacts on things and people you touch just by being kind, accountable, and trustworthy, to bring advancement. Impact is like sowing and reaping. The way you impact people around you today manifests and materializes with time. Early positive impact on children is important; mindsets are formed by what people hear, see, or practice at home (Ps. 127:3–4). Negative experiences can affect future actions whereby individuals may feel very uncomfortable reaching out to be stagnated (Prov. 11:29). People may struggle with making an impact when their exposures are limited, territorial, and biased. Nonetheless, impacting others is ingrained in every human as a stakeholder to improve our surroundings. Impact is a cyclical chain reaction of valuing others to value lives and relationships for encouragement and accountability; this transcends into changing habits that are counterproductive. Words, actions, and character are an important elemental mixture that may produce negative or positive impacts. The mixture of positive variance is God's desire for health and wealth for all (Eph. 6:8). It is as simple as doing things like giving a glass of water to a thirsty person, answering the call of a needy patient, and taking time to give the right directions to a stranger (Gal. 6:9).

Everyone is a shareholder on planet earth, full of riches and wealth, if only people could take time to understand the fundamental secrets of positive impact (Prov. 8:18). The impetus for becoming famous is not by hiding your talents, refusing to make contributions, or seeking power by any means. Anything that shifts your focus from considering others as valuable and deserving your impact will never bring sustained wealth and happiness. Most people are experiencing failure, poverty, and un-fulfillment for failing to reach out and touch others positively. The wealth, growth, and development of any society depend on people's positive impact on one another—it is a key for wealth. It is a dual portal to give and receive impact, whereby all participants blend their best and worst times to come up with a good mix to benefit all. How? Someone's positive impact at the zenith provides remedies for others at their lowest moments (Luke 22:31–32). Immunization, advancement in medicine, and other high-tech aspects are a few examples of such an impact. It is like a lineup of dominoes whereby the first receives an impact and falls back to touch the next, and the next, with a synchronized, beautiful sound for the enjoyment of billions. Make an impact to be heard.

The loud voices of the people you had impacted in your journey echoes to celebrate you.

About the Author

D r. Love Otuechere is inspirational writer with over 500 readers of her weekly columns in Boston metropolis.

She is president of Ibo Cultural women group, promoting "it takes a village to raise a child" whereby the youths are mentored and encouraged to advance purposefully in life. She is an author of "The Journal of a Champion." She is a life alumni member of Indiana University, Indiana, having attended both Bloomington and Indianapolis campuses. She attends Foursquare Gospel Church in Hyde Park, Massachusetts, actively involved in missions, DYS and Nursing Home Project Compassion teams.